ANN ARBOR
FRESH!

Recipes and Stories from the Ann Arbor Farmers' Market
and the Kerrytown Historic District

ANN ARBOR

FRESH!

Recipes and Stories from the Ann Arbor Farmers' Market
and the Kerrytown Historic District

by
Raquel B. Agranoff and Lois Kane

An AGRAKANE, Inc. Publication, Ann Arbor, Michigan, USA

An AGRAKANE, Inc. publication
Library of Congress Catalog Card Number: 98-93340
ISBN 0-9666191-0-2

Manufactured in the United States of America
First Printing: 1998
Copyright ©1998 AGRAKANE, Inc., Ann Arbor, Michigan, USA

To order copies of *Ann Arbor Fresh!* send $20.45 (for Michigan residents, $21.38) to:
Kitchen Port, 415 North Fifth Avenue, Ann Arbor, MI. 48104
or to order by phone and pay by credit card, call 1-800-832-7678
(Postage for orders outside the U.S. is somewhat higher)

Book design by Will Agranoff Design, Seattle, WA

DEDICATION

This book is dedicated to our husbands,

Bernie Agranoff and Gordy Kane—with love and gratitude.

ALSO BY RAQUEL B. AGRANOFF

Cooking in Porcelain

Risotto, Paellas and Other Rice Dishes

ACKNOWLEDGMENTS

A sincere thanks for the skill, good nature,
and helpful suggestions from all the
food testers and tasters:

Julie Agranoff, Ximena Antunes, Oscar de Armas,
Nancy Asin, MariCarmen Davies, Mercedes Ferre,
Ana Mari Greeven, Elizabeth Moore, Helen Pancoast,
Jean Rivkin, Grace Shackman, and Elizabeth Warner.

The authors are also grateful to the following
persons and groups for their kind interest
and knowledgeable suggestions:

The Ann Arbor City Market Commission,
The Ann Arbor Farmers' Market Growers' Association,
Bernard Agranoff, Lisa Bergman, Jim Edwards, Leslie
Gresham, John Hilton, Gordon Kane,
Jan Longone, Louisa Pieper, Joe O'Neal, Henry
Pollack, John Rasmusson, Dennis Rice, Maxine
Rosasco, and Grace Shackman.

Special thanks to Mary Matthews, who helped in
many ways; to Rose Grant who, as always,
has made the finest possible cookbook index;
and to Will Agranoff for his graphic
design expertise, patience and humor.

TABLE OF CONTENTS

The word "appetizer" has been used to describe any finger food eaten before a meal, and is also synonymous with "hors d'oeuvre". The recipes in this chapter are mostly "sit-down" recipes, with a few "stand-ups", too.

Soups and salads comprise the very heart of market cooking. Here are thick soups, basic stocks, and tingling salsas to excite the palate.

A simple boiled beef dinner, trendy squash enchiladas, and smoked salmon cakes, are just a few of the many entrees inspired by market and artisan shops.

The wonderful thing about side dishes is that they can also masquerade as lunch, brunch or appetizers. Here are seventeen with that adaptability.

PREFACE

How this book came about.

White peaches, fresh morels, fiddlehead ferns, golden raspberries, puffballs—these are just a few of the exotic edible glories of the outdoor and indoor markets in the Kerrytown Historic Market District. Even everyday fruits and vegetables are given the same care and attention as their fancy cousins. Flowers, jewelry, ceramics, furniture, candles, clothing, fish, meat, coffee, tea, beer, bread, and cheese are also on hand. The Ann Arbor Farmers' Market is not simply a twice a week place where we savor, sniff, and taste. It is a place to greet friends, to plan a meal, to buy a treat, to meander. From spring, when we choose our fat (or thin) asparagus spears one by one and linger over the first tender leaves of lettuce, through summer with its aroma of sweet strawberries, until the last days of fall, when the squashes, multi-colored peppers, and crisp apples appear, we are the fortunate beneficiaries of bountiful harvests.

The Ann Arbor Farmers' Market has been part of my life since I came to Ann Arbor in 1960. I found the market reminiscent of those I had seen in places I had lived in earlier—in Boston, Munich, and Manila, among others. I had watched Kerrytown's birth next to the Farmers' Market, when, in 1969, I became the founding manager of Kitchen Port, the kitchen supply store that's still there. Kerrytown soon proved itself to be a perfect fit with the outdoor market. Gradually, produce, cheese, fish, and baked goods joined Kitchen Port. Then in 1977, four friends and I started the Moveable Feast, a catering and bakery operation in Kerrytown. In the very early morning hours on market days, I would make my way through the dark to our basement kitchen to bake bread. The hustle of the market days became a part of my life. Though I was a novice on the scene, the farmers had been coming year after year, arriving in their trucks, setting up their stalls, selling their produce, taking down their stalls, and starting all over again the next Wednesday or Saturday. Not only had they been coming to the market all through their lives, but many of them as youngsters, had accompanied their parents, and even their grandparents to Ann Arbor on market days. The interviews we conducted with the market growers and shop owners for the preparation of this book revealed their commitment and deepened our understanding of their lives and their work.

Most of us do appreciate and recognize the wonderful choices that the market brings us: the freshest, the greatest variety, and the most tenderly cared for produce available during the season. The growers can practically cite the genealogy of each item they sell, and they take pride in each berry, every potato, and tomato. None of their produce is waxed or prewrapped. Although many of the growers do not emphasize the fact that their produce is organically grown, in most in-stances it is. The small farm grower has control over what goes into the ground and onto the plants. Growers have responded to the requests of the public for more exotic and unusual produce. Asian vegetables are displayed side by side with puffballs and golden raspberries. Lemongrass perfumes the air next to the maple sugar stand. Every herb imaginable is available, along with advice on what to do with it. Do we ever fully realize how lucky we are?

The indoor market at Kerrytown is also bursting with fresh fish, meat, and produce, coupled with knowledgeable advice and pride of product. Here we can find just about anything we need to prepare a meal, simple or elegant. As the demand has been established, the response has met the challenge. There is a depth and richness of food that is the equal of older cultures.

Bread so satisfying that you can make a meal of it. (Maybe with a little bit of butter?) Cheese and wine and smoked salmon so good that you just can't keep it a secret.

It seemed to be the right time to write this book. Not only do we in Ann Arbor have access to the riches of the food world, but the right mix of people are here to appreciate it. What a lucky coincidence that I bumped into Lois! Even though I had known her for years, our paths had not crossed for a long time. When I told her what I was planning, something clicked in both of us, and our collaboration has been a joy.

Although we have both conducted the interviews, Lois has written them, as well as the introduction. Her years of experience on the *Ann Arbor Observer* come through in the seamless, expertly told tales she weaves.

Some of the recipes have been provided by the growers, and I have supplied the rest, which are either original, or classic ones which have been updated. All of the recipes that are not flat out simple have been tested.

About 20 recipes in this book were generously shared with us by the growers or by folks involved with the market. Most of the recipes utilize ingredients found in the Kerrytown Market area, outdoors or indoors. That is why, for example, there is a recipe for prickly pear sorbet. You will find this cactus pear fruit at Zingerman's Practical Produce in Kerrytown, just as you will find bitter melon and raspberries in the Farmers' Market, and corresponding recipes in this book to utilize them. The dazzling array of specialty foods in Zingerman's Deli, and the emphasis on local products and natural foods of the Peoples' Food Co-op also inspired me. For all the recipes, I had a common requirement: they must have a deeply satisfying and comforting taste. They didn't have to be unique or elaborate, but I do admit to a personal preference for recipes that are structured. They may consist of several components, which, when assembled, create a whole that is better than the sum of its parts. (That preference explains, for example, a recipe for chicken strudel.) It is my hope that the reader-cooks will have fun, learn a little, and feel that they have a bit of Ann Arbor in their kitchen when they use this book.

There is a chapter on cooking basics which is an explanation of techniques and why I suggest using certain ingredients. It is almost a sampler of my cooking philosophy: use the best quality ingredients available, follow instructions, but be inventive — and above all, take pleasure in what you are creating.

Raquel B. Agranoff

INTRODUCTION

Why Farmers Are Retailers and Retailers Are Artisans.

A big chunk of Washtenaw County's romance is found in Ann Arbor's Farmers' Market and Kerrytown area, site of restaurants, shops, entertainment places—including the Kerrytown Concert House—and the oldest element, the Ann Arbor Farmers' Market itself.

The market originated in 1919, a few blocks away from its current site. Under the aegis of a federation of local women's organizations, farmers began selling their produce on the steps of the grand old Victorian city hall, located on the block bordered by Main, Huron, Ann, and North Fourth now occupied by the Washtenaw County Courthouse. That market set the rule that distinguishes the Ann Arbor Farmers' Market to this day: anything sold at the market must have been produced by its vendor.

In 1921, the city took over the market's administration. As the number of participating farmers grew, stalls lined the streets along Ann and North Fourth Avenue. Appropriately called the "curb market," the informal arrangement inevitably led to crowded sidewalks and tangled traffic problems. In 1931, former mayor Gottlob Luick remedied the situation by donating the land where the market is located today, between North Fourth Avenue and Detroit Street. The land was part of Luick's lumberyard and next to a grain mill and a feed store, both frequented by farmers. In the 1960's, as the area became urbanized, the farm-oriented businesses closed or moved, leaving their large brick buildings standing empty and unused.

Art Carpenter, a local lawyer, visionary, and romantic, fell in love with the simple structures and saw their potential. In 1969, he and a group of investors set to work turning the empty shells into a complex of shops and restaurants. He named it "Kerrytown" to honor County Kerry, the birthplace of his Irish mother-in-law. In addition to food shops and restaurants, the Kerrytown complex now houses a florist, art galleries and craft shops, a candle store, a custom invitation shop, a beauty salon, a furniture store, and several delightful women's clothing shops.

But as Kerrytown was developing, the Farmers' Market was struggling. In 1979, a local paper, *The Alchemist*, ran a long article titled "Can the Farmers' Market Survive Old Age and Modern Times?" and in 1988 the *Ann Arbor Observer* ran one called, "Hard Times for the Farmers' Market." The recurrent problem that prompted both articles is the still-threatening possibility that small farming will disappear altogether under the coarse thumb of giant agribusiness.

During World War II, with rationing and the disruption of food supplies, the Farmers' Market had thrived and every stall was occupied. But as the nature of agriculture began to change, the number of area farmers was already declining, and competition from specialty produce stores, bringing in products from farther afield, was taking a toll. Also, increasing governmental health regulation began to affect the kinds of products farmers were allowed to sell: gone now are dairy products, fresh meats, and all baked goods except those produced in commercial kitchens. By 1988 the number of vendors at the market had fallen to 75 from a high of 126 in 1976.

Despite the continual attrition among area farmers, and despite the growing number of splendid, but competitive, food stores, the Farmers' Market is clearly on the rebound. Ten percent of the stalls are allotted to craftspeople; although they are not profiled in this food-oriented book, their ceramics, textiles, jewelry, and other crafts brighten and enliven the market. The 144 stalls allotted to farmers are always full, and there is great demand for more. Consequently, the Market Commission hopes to expand the market when the land now occupied by a frame dwelling on North Fifth Avenue becomes available.

For customers, the greatest lure of the market is probably the pure sensual and communal pleasure of simply being there. But will farmers continue to fill the stalls? Why do they come?

Market days are extremely difficult for the vendors. They spend the day—and often a good part of the night before—gathering, washing, and bundling their produce and flowers. They get up in the wee hours in order to arrive at the market before 6 a.m. Often it's miserably cold or rainy. They stand for most of the day. They must be congenial no matter what the circumstances or how trying the customer. Why do they do it? Because they love it. The economics of the business determine what kind of people will be successful farmers in our non-agrarian culture. Unlike yesteryear's relatively isolated farmers leading quiet lives on family places, today's successful farmer-vendors are people who enjoy the gregarious hubbub of the marketplace.

Farmers Are Retailers

Growers who bring their produce to market are called "truck farmers." The alternative is "cash-crop farming," in which an entire large crop, such as wheat or soybeans, is sold to a grain elevator or other distributor. Cash-crop farming requires a lot of land, equipment, and hired labor, and is vulnerable to market and weather variations. Many of the Ann Arbor Farmers' Market farmers grew up in cash-crop families, and a few still do cash-crop farming in addition to their truck garden produce. Truck farmer Leola Wasem of Wasem's Orchards says, "You either have to be huge, or very small so you don't need help. We can't afford to pay help. If I paid someone for what we're doing, we couldn't sell for what we're selling for."

Truck farmers also sell produce to local stores. The People's Food Co-op, for example, buys quite a lot. Even big chains like

Meijer buy some local produce. But produce markup is small, so to survive, small growers have to be their own retailers. Some of the growers have stands or shops at their farms; Ralph Snow operates a buffet breakfast restaurant at his farm in Mason every winter. But the Farmers' Market is a necessary part of their livelihoods.

The farmers fall roughly into three categories. Most grew up in farm families. Others are environmental and health idealists who take time to educate the public about organic farming and land preservation. A small number have chosen the pastoral life as a post-retirement career. Many of the farmers have full-time paying jobs; they say that perhaps they could get by day to day on their farm incomes, but that they could not afford such benefits as retirement savings and health insurance.

Most of the farmers, even the ones who don't mention it, practice organic farming techniques to some extent. What they all have in common is love for what they're doing and pride in doing it well. Most practice good land management. Al and Florence Kierczak are standout examples.

"I never fool with bugs. I don't have any," Al told us. "I have no weed killer on here at all. Never. Never. The only thing I spray is potatoes, and this year I didn't have to do that." We visited the Kierczaks at the end of July 1997. Their long, narrow twenty-acre truck garden is near Milan, a few miles south of Ann Arbor. To us, the landscape looked flat and simple—black dirt, green plants, big blue sky. To Al Kierczak, it is obviously a complex patchwork of rises and dips, loamy wet places and dry sandy ones, spots where pickling cucumbers can lie low and spots that are better for the 160,000 gladiolas that stand almost as tall as Al himself.

"Look down," he said. We were standing on ground as white as paper: sand. In the last Ice Age, the Milan area was part of Lake Erie's bed. A short distance away is a transition area that looks like chocolate ripple ice cream, where the sand swirls into a patch of black earth; over a way there's a large field planted with rye. Al plants rye and plows it under for two seasons in a row, naturally reinvigorating and fertilizing the earth before he plants it again with produce for market. "It makes the earth feel warmer [to the hand]," he said.

By judicious trenching, Kierczak has made a sort of natural irrigation system that allows large areas of his farm to thrive without watering. Even his machinery is recycled and adapted; he has fitted ancient tractors with ingenious devices. One is a planter he adapted so Florence can sit on the tractor and simply pour seed through a tube. Another device raises potato plant leaves, making it easier to lift the potatoes out of the ground.

One of the joys of working on this book was visiting the Kierczaks, and later the Dieterles, at their farms. But how long will this kind of farming last? Grower Alex Nemeth says there used to be twenty-five farms between his fruit orchard and Ypsilanti; today there are three. Joyce Kapnick recently sold part of her orchard to a residential developer. Other farmers say they regularly get enticing offers for their land. Farm costs are rising; farm income is not.

But Peter Stark thinks he can survive by augmenting market sales with catalog sales, and the Merkel farms in Chelsea will survive because the third generation has husbands at work and wives running the greenhouse and gardens. Like all good retailers, these farmers are adapting to the marketplace. In response to recent demand, many have added baby vegetables—tiny carrots, diminutive summer squashes, and little pea shoots—that make lovely appetizer trays, and exotic vegetables such as Chinese greens and edible blooms.

A city-appointed Market Commission oversees the market. Maxine Rosasco has been the market master since 1987. Beginning at 7 a.m. on market mornings, she assigns stalls and watches over the bustling area. The little red brick market office is always busy. It's a place of refuge for the vendors, who come in to have a bite to eat, to warm up, or just to take a quiet break. Customers come in to ask directions (or they may be looking for the restrooms across the way), to fetch or bring in lost items, to purchase shopping bags, or to ask for a Band-Aid. The phone rings almost constantly with messages for stall holders and queries about market hours. We are so impressed by Maxine's dedication to the market that Ricky has named one of the recipes in this book—"Pears Maxine"—in her honor.

Retailers Are Artisans

Just as some farmers do double duty as retailers, some shop owners do double duty as artisans. Historically, shops arose as places where artisans traded goods—first for other goods, then for money. Gradually, with the growth of department stores and supermarkets, retail shops became places where vendors simply took goods made elsewhere and passed them along to consumers. The Kerrytown area food shops remain in the artisan-owner tradition. Most of them create or add value to the food products they sell. The Kerrytown area food retailers are old-fashioned craftspeople disguised by modern refrigeration.

Brewbakers brews beer and soft drinks in high-tech equipment and bakes fabulous breads in an old-fashioned brick oven; T. R. Durham of Tracklements produces incomparable smoked fishes and meats; Monahan's Fish Market brings us the freshest and highest quality fish possible; Sparrow Meat Market cuts and sells the best meats, many of them prepared for the oven with delicious stuffings; Zingerman's Practical Produce carries Zingerman's Bakehouse breads and pastries along with produce from around the world. In the Kerrytown Market there is a wine and cheese shop, a coffee and tea shop, and a distinguished kitchenware store. Across Detroit Street, the astonishing Zingerman's deli searches out the finest food craftspeople in the world and treats their offerings with a reverence that is advancing the cause of fine food artisans everywhere. The People's Food Co-op, half a block south of the Farmers' Market, promotes and sells organic food products, thus supporting local organic growers, bread bakers, and food preservers. The Co-op also carries kitchen necessities from baking powder to washing powder, so it's possible to do nearly complete grocery shopping without leaving the Farmers' Market/Kerrytown area.

ANN ARBOR FRESH!

APPETIZERS

A meal can start with finger foods ("hors d'oeuvre"), which are passed around to accompany drinks and eaten casually while standing, or it can begin with a first course served at the table. It seems to me that over the years, the ubiquitous chip-and-dip or carrot sticks for cocktails have more accurately come to be thought of as different from the first course that we enjoy eating while seated at the table. The recipes in this chapter are mostly for "sit-down" appetizers, with a few "stand-ups" thrown in. Salty, smooth, perhaps garlicky, they serve to usher the diner on to the next course by piquing the appetite and satisfying the hunger without dulling the palate. Cheddar cheese biscuits melt on the tongue and slices of vegetable terrine bedazzle the eye. Cool, fresh tomatoes and okra whet the appetite for something savory, and shrimp toast and broccoli timbale call for something crunchy to follow. These recipes will, I hope, make it easy and fun to construct a full menu, but they can also be used as part of a large buffet, or as components of a light supper.

CAPONATA OF ZUCCHINI

YIELD: 6-8 CUPS

10 medium zucchini
(4-5 inches long), washed
and cut into 1 inch dice

1/3 cup extra virgin olive oil

2 cups coarsely chopped celery

2 cups coarsely chopped
 fennel bulb

3 cups peeled, seeded, and
chopped fresh tomatoes

3/4 cup capers, drained

1/2 cup chopped black
oil-cured olives

4 cloves garlic, minced or pressed

3/4 cup Balsamic vinegar

2 tablespoons granulated sugar

1 red bell pepper, roasted, diced
(see "Basics")

1/2 cup toasted pine nuts
(see "Basics")

1/2 teaspoon salt and freshly
ground pepper to taste

When you have exhausted every zucchini recipe you have ever made, and the sight of one more zucchini makes your eyes glaze over, give it another chance with this approach. Caponata originated in Sicily, and is usually made with eggplant, anchovies, onions, tomatoes, and capers, all cooked together with olive oil and vinegar and garnished with roasted pine nuts.

Although we substitute zucchini for the eggplant here, the dish retains the mellowness of its Sicilian ancestor. This is a great accompaniment to lamb, or a filling for an omelet. And it makes a terrific, albeit unorthodox, sandwich filling.

Heat oil in a large (14 inch) sauté pan, and add the diced zucchini. Sauté until light brown, then remove from the pan with a slotted spoon. Add the chopped celery and fennel and sauté until tender, about 5 minutes. Lower heat and add the chopped tomato, and cook for another 5 minutes. Return the zucchini to the pan and add the capers, black olives, garlic, Balsamic vinegar, and sugar. Simmer for another 5 minutes. Some liquid will have exuded from the cooked vegetables. Drain off this liquid, reduce it by 2/3 in another pan, and add it back to the drained vegetables. Mix in the diced red pepper and toasted pine nuts. Taste for seasoning and add salt and pepper. Cool and refrigerate the mixture, or let it come to room temperature and serve. You can make this mixture as much as 4 or 5 days ahead.

TIP: IF YOU PREFER YOUR PINE NUTS CRUNCHY, DO NOT ADD THEM UNTIL JUST BEFORE SERVING.

CHEDDAR CHEESE BISCUITS

Do you ever crave just a little bite of something that's cheesy, but not too cheesy? Spicy, but not too spicy? Easy to make? Here it is. This recipe uses Cheddar cheese, but you can substitute any other sharp cheese, or combination of sharp cheeses, such as Gruyère or Monterey Jack. It is also good made with a strong blue cheese, such as Maytag Blue, Stilton, or Gorgonzola. Be sure to cream the butter and cheese well together, a blended result which will melt-in-your-mouth.

3/4 cup unsalted butter, room temperature

3 cups sharp Cheddar cheese, shredded

1 tablespoon dried mustard powder

1/4 teaspoon cayenne pepper

1 tablespoon chopped fresh dill (optional)

1 1/2 cups all-purpose flour

Heat oven to 350 degrees. Cream the softened butter and shredded cheese together until they are fully blended. It can be done in the bowl of a food processor; continue by adding the rest of the ingredients and processing until they are combined. You can also combine the ingredients with an electric mixer, using the flat whip. Do not use a whisk. The batter is too thick, and should you manage to get a whisk through the mass, it will beat air into it, and that is not what you want. Now do one of two things: either roll the mixture out into two thin sausage ropes, and refrigerate for at least an hour until they are cold enough to slice into 1/4 inch thick slices, or place the mixture in a very large (16 inch) pastry bag, use a large fluted tube, and pipe biscuits about 1 1/2 inches in diameter onto an ungreased baking sheet. Bake 8-10 minutes, or until they are slightly brown and the middle is dry.

Tip: IT MAY BE DIFFICULT TO PIPE THE DOUGH FROM A PASTRY BAG, AS THE MIXTURE IS VERY DENSE. YOU MAY WANT TO FILL THE PASTRY BAG AND LET IT SIT AT ROOM TEMPERATURE FOR A HALF HOUR OR SO BEFORE YOU START PIPING.

CAULIFLOWER, EGGPLANT, AND ZUCCHINI TIMBALE

SERVES 8

1 medium cauliflower

3 cloves garlic, minced or pressed

1 teaspoon salt

1 tablespoon white truffle oil

1 eggplant, about 9 inches long

1 zucchini, about 6 inches long

vegetable spray

1 tablespoon roasted, ground cumin seed (see "Basics")

salt and freshly ground pepper to taste

Here we are again: simplicity elevated to elegance, an unexpected twist that presents vegetables in an unusual form. A touch of white truffle oil is added. Eggplant is thinly sliced and roasted briefly until it is limp. The vegetables combine to fill individual timbales. The roasted red pepper sauce is gorgeous with the muted olive and white tones of the unmolded timbale.

Cut or break apart the cauliflower into florets no bigger than golf ball size. Steam them over simmering water, covered, until soft and easily pierced with a fork (about 10 minutes). Drain and purée cauliflower in a food processor. Add the garlic, salt, and truffle oil. Taste and adjust seasoning. Set aside, or refrigerate if you intend to complete the recipe later.

Heat oven to 350 degrees. Coat a baking sheet with vegetable spray. Slice unpeeled eggplant and zucchini into 1/4 inch slices from stem to blossom end. Lay the slices in a colander, salt them liberally, and let them sit for at least 15 minutes to draw out some of their natural liquid, which would interfere with proper cooking. If the eggplant has exuded lots of liquid, squeeze the slices gently before blotting them. Arrange eggplant slices on the oiled baking sheet and roast for 5 minutes on each side until they are pliable. It is not necessary to roast the zucchini slices. Sprinkle the ground cumin seed, salt, and pepper over the eggplant slices as they cool.

Brush 8 individual timbale molds, or custard cups, with olive oil. Line the molds with overlapping slices of the eggplant and zucchini. You might have to trim the ends of the slices. Leave enough overhanging to flip over the filled timbale. Spoon in the cauliflower purée to the top of the mold. Flip the ends of the strips of eggplant and zucchini over the filled mold. Store in refrigerator. When you are ready to cook the timbales, heat the oven to 375 degrees. Place molds in a roasting pan and pour in boiling water until it reaches 2/3 of the way up the mold. (To prevent spilling, it's best to do this when the pan is already sitting on the oven rack.) Cover the molds with a piece of aluminum foil, and bake for approximately 20 minutes. Alternatively, you may place them on a rack and steam them in a covered pot over boiling water for 20 minutes. When you remove the timbales from the water or rack, transfer them with a large spatula. Turn them upside down on a serving dish or plate to catch any juices. Serve with Roasted Red Pepper Sauce (See "Sauces").

CRAB BUNDLES

SERVES 8

This recipe is best when it is made with fresh lump crab meat, free of cartilage, and not previously frozen. You will find it chilled in the fresh food section of your supermarket or fish store. It is expensive, and when you spend this much you want to make sure that you have a superior product from a place like Monahan's at Kerrytown to provide you not only with superb crab, but expert advice on how to cook and store it. Really fresh crab in season is full of flavor, and worth waiting for to include in this outstanding dish.

Heat oven to 350 degrees. Heat olive oil in a medium-sized sauté pan and cook the sliced leek and garlic until wilted. Add the curry powder, cumin, and paprika and mix briefly. Remove from heat and add all remaining ingredients except the filo dough, butter, and chives. Place one square of filo dough on a wooden board or a flat counter. (Keep the rest of the filo covered with a damp cloth. It dries out very quickly, so work as fast as you can.) Brush with melted butter. Place another square of filo dough diagonally on top of the first, making an eight-pointed star. Place a heaping 1/3 cup of filling in the center of the filo. Pull up the eight corners of the filo to meet in the center above the mound of filling and twist slightly. The bundle will resemble a purse or a pouch. Tie a chive or scallion "string" around the neck of the pouch, making a bow. Brush bundles with melted butter and place on a baking sheet lined with parchment or oiled waxed paper. Bake about 35 minutes, or until lightly browned. Serve with Roasted Red Pepper Sauce (see "Sauces").

TIP: FOR AN INTERESTING VARIATION YOU CAN REPLACE 6 OUNCES OF THE CRAB MEAT WITH RAW SHRIMP, COOKED LOBSTER, OR DICED RAW MONKFISH.

---

1 tablespoon olive oil

1 leek, white part only, cleaned and cut across into thin rings

3 cloves pressed garlic

2 teaspoons curry powder

1 teaspoon roasted, ground cumin (see "Basics")

1/2 teaspoon sweet paprika

12 ounces fresh crab meat

1/3 cup frozen peas, not thawed

1/2 teaspoon mustard powder

1/2 cup cooked corn

1 teaspoon fresh minced ginger root

1 large egg, beaten

salt and freshly ground pepper to taste

16 sheets of filo dough, each 8 1/2 inches square

1/4 cup melted butter

8 chives or scallion greens about 10 inches long, blanched

FISH TIMBALES

=== SERVES 6 ===

1 cup salmon or tuna

1 cup soft bread crumbs

1 cup mashed potatoes, rice, or hominy

1/4 teaspoon salt

1/4 teaspoon paprika

This recipe for a fish timbale appears opposite the Forward page of Virginia Hammond's cookbook, *Home on the Range*. It lurks behind the picture of Virginia, who is made up and dressed to look like a benevolent grandmother. The recipe is 80 years or more old, and it caught my eye because I realized that it is still a practical way to make a fish timbale. (See the Broccoli Timbale recipe in the "Side Dishes" chapter for more about a timbale.) The fish can be salmon or tuna, according to the recipe. We have chosen to test it using canned salmon, as this is almost always on hand. Here is the recipe as it appears in the book, with thanks to Virginia. (We have added the text in parentheses.)

Heat oven to 375 degrees. Mix ingredients together. Pour into greased molds and place on a rack in a shallow pan. Pour boiling water half way up the sides of the pan, place in preheated oven. and bake until firm. (About 30 minutes, using 6 ounce molds. A sharp knife inserted into the middle of the timbale should come out clean.) Serve with a béchamel sauce (see "Sauces") to which you have added puréed peas. Use 3 tablespoons of cooked, puréed peas to 1 cup of béchamel sauce.

FRESH VEGETABLE TERRINE

This seems rather fussy to make, and it is, a little. But it is so beautiful and so tasty that it is definitely worth it. Pack the vegetables close together so the sliced terrine will look gorgeous and jewel-like when you cut through it. Serve it as part of a buffet, or as a first course.

Using a small bowl, soften the gelatin in the white wine. Place bowl over boiling water to further dissolve the powder. (Be careful not to allow the bottom of the bowl to sit in the water, since it will cook the gelatin.) It takes about 10 minutes to dissolve the gelatin to its clear state. Combine the cream cheese, goat cheese, and cottage cheese in the bowl of a food processor or mixer and beat together until well combined. If the mixture seems thick, add the optional 1/2 cup milk. Add the minced garlic and dill and mix thoroughly. While the machine is running, add the dissolved gelatin.

Line a loaf pan or terrine with parchment paper, plastic wrap or waxed paper. Spread or pour into the pan enough of the mixed cheese mixture to reach a depth of 1 inch. Arrange some asparagus along the top of the filling, spears close together. Add another layer of the cheese mixture, and arrange some of the remaining vegetables over the top. Try to keep the vegetable pieces quite close together. Continue layering the cheese and vegetables in this manner, ending with a layer of the cheese mixture on top. Place another piece of parchment, plastic wrap or waxed paper over all, and cover with aluminum foil. Fit a weight directly on top of the terrine so it is actually on the filling, and not resting on the edges of the container. Add more weight, such as cans of food on their sides, or a narrow bread board, making sure the terrine is evenly weighted. Place weighted terrine in refrigerator. Chill the terrine for at least 2 hours. Unmold and slice carefully with a very sharp knife dipped in hot water.

Serve with a few roasted, salted pecan halves and a teaspoon of olive oil poured over the top of each slice.

1 envelope unflavored gelatin

1/2 cup white wine

6 ounces low fat whipped cream cheese

12 ounces low fat creamy goat cheese

2 cups low fat cottage cheese

1/2 cup low fat milk (optional)

4 cloves garlic, minced

1 cup fresh dill

12-18 asparagus stalks, blanched, cut into 3 inch lengths

1 roasted red pepper, cut in 1/2 inch wide strips (see "Basics")

1 roasted yellow pepper, cut into 1/2 inch wide strips

12 whole radishes, blanched, cut in half

6 scallions, cut into 3 inch lengths (white and green parts)

1 cup roasted pecan halves (see "Basics")

2 tablespoons extra virgin olive oil

GATEAU OF TUNA TARTARE

== SERVES 6 ==

2 yellow, orange, or red peppers

4 tablespoons extra virgin olive oil, divided

1 or 2 large potatoes, peeled and sliced into 1/4 inch rounds

2-3 tablespoons canola oil

1 pound raw yellow fin tuna

4 scallions, sliced into thin rings, white and green parts

3 tablespoons toasted sesame seeds (see "Basics")

2 tablespoons chili oil

2 tablespoons sesame oil

2 tablespoons soy sauce

1 tablespoon Japanese horseradish powder (wasabi)

2 tablespoons water

6 tablespoons crème frâiche or yogurt

1/2 avocado

12 chive stalks

This is a recipe for the brave. For those of us who enjoy steak tartare, or Japanese sashimi or sushi, it is a natural leap to eating raw tuna presented this way. For those of us who think eating raw fish is just too unusual and is best left to those cultures who already appreciate it,— be adventuresome. The sesame and chili oils, along with the soy sauce, present a finish to the tuna which is absolutely a marriage made in gourmand heaven. Okay, it's not for everyone, but if you feel daring, give it a try. The tuna should be of the highest quality, carefully pampered from the sea to the market. You can find the freshest, sushi quality tuna at Monahan's in Kerrytown or at other reliable fish markets in your area. (If you really don't like the idea of eating raw tuna, try the recipe with a mixture of lightly poached salmon and gravlax). Wasabi, a Japanese horseradish powder, is also available at Monahan's, and at some supermarkets. Mix the powder with small amounts of water until you have a spoonable consistency. Be careful— it is very strong, and could "blow your head off"!

Remove and discard seeds from peppers and purée the peppers with 2 tablespoons of the oil until the mixture is smooth. Set aside. Slice potatoes into 18 even 1/4 inch rounds and sauté them in the remaining 2 tablespoons olive oil. Remove from pan, and blot well on paper towels. Set aside. Using a sharp knife, dice raw tuna into 1/4 inch pieces and combine with the sesame seeds, chili and sesame oils, and soy sauce.

Construct each gateau by alternating slices of potato and tuna mixture, using a potato slice on the bottom, one in the middle, and one on top. Mix the Japanese horseradish with 2 tablespoons water and combine with the crème frâiche or yogurt. Cut the avocado into 1/4 inch dice. Arrange each gateau on a plate, surrounded by alternating mounds of pepper purée, wasabi-crème frâiche, and avocado. Criss-cross two chives on the top of each gateau.

Tip: Instead of sautéing the potato slices, you can steam or boil them in a small amount of salted water. This should take about 5 minutes. Drain and blot them well before proceeding with the recipe.

Tip: Freezing raw fish should get rid of any parasites that might have lingered. Partial thawing makes it easier to cut into even dice.

SHRIMP TOASTS

One of the nice things about this recipe, since the mixture will be coarsely puréed, is that the size of the shrimp does not matter. This means that you can use less expensive, small shrimp. This appetizer has a crunchy texture and it can be made ahead and reheated in the oven. It is necessary, however, to follow the frying instructions. Do not try to sauté the toasts in a small amount of oil. They absorb too much oil this way, and taste heavy and greasy.

Slice bread into 1/4" slices. Purée the remaining ingredients, except the sesame seeds and vegetable oil. Spread each bread slice with the mixture, then sprinkle with the sesame seeds. In a 2 quart pot, heat oil to 350 degrees. (You can also use a deep fryer for this.) Place toasts, filled side down, in the hot oil and fry for one minute. Turn toasts to the other side, and fry another minute. Drain on paper towels. Serve hot.

TIP: THESE MAY BE REHEATED IN A 350 DEGREE OVEN. WASABI IS A GREEN POWDER MOST OFTEN SERVED WITH JAPANESE SUSHI. IT MUST BE MIXED WITH WATER TO A PASTE-LIKE CONSISTENCY. IT IS AVAILABLE IN MOST ASIAN GROCERY STORES AND SOME SUPERMARKETS.

1 slender loaf French bread

2 cups peeled and deveined shrimp (size doesn't matter)

2 eggs

2 tablespoons cream

4 dried shiitake mushrooms, reconstituted (see "Basics")

2 tablespoons soy sauce

1 cup bean sprouts

2 scallions, green and white parts, chopped fine

2 cloves garlic, finely chopped

1 tablespoon grated fresh ginger

1 tablespoon hot sesame oil

1/2 teaspoon Japanese horseradish powder (wasabi)

1 cup white sesame seeds

4 cups vegetable oil

SHRIMP & PORK STUFFED GRAPE LEAVES

YIELD: 2 DOZEN

1/2 pound peeled and deveined shrimp, chopped finely

1/2 pound lean ground pork

1 tablespoon chopped flat-leafed parsley

1 tablespoon grated fresh ginger

2 tablespoons chopped cilantro

1/4 cup minced onion

3 cloves garlic, minced

1 tablespoon chopped fresh tarragon

2 red bell peppers, roasted and diced (see "Basics")

1 teaspoon salt and freshly ground pepper to taste

24 marinated grape leaves, rinsed

I think of this recipe every summer when I pass through the parking lot of the Farmers' Market where beautiful wild grape leaves cover the sides of an old fence. They are just waiting to be plucked, marinated, and filled. But you can also find canned, marinated grape leaves quite easily these days, either in the supermarkets, in the international section, or in one of the many Middle Eastern markets that dot the city. For this recipe, use any size shrimp you like, whatever is least expensive, since you will be chopping them up, anyway.

Combine all of the above ingredients except the grape leaves. Divide mixture into 4 parts. Blot the rinsed grape leaves with paper toweling and lay them out flat, six at a time, underside up. Spread 1/4 of the filling across the center of each of the six leaves. Fold in the sides of each leaf to the center, and roll up tightly, into a tube shape. Set the filled leaves on a tray or rack over 2 inches of boiling water in a saucepan and steam, covered, on top of stove for 8-10 minutes. Serve plain, or with a béchamel sauce flavored with 2 tablespoons chopped fresh tarragon and 1/2 teaspoon dried tarragon (see "Sauces").

BROCCOLI TIMBALE

═══ SERVES 6 ═══

What is a timbale? It is a cylindrical mold, tapered slightly at one end, filled with a savory or sweet mixture and cooked in a water bath in the oven. It is usually custard-based, but the form itself can be used to mold simple purées or even cooked rice. Small oven-proof custard cups or soufflé molds may be substituted for the classic timbale shape. A timbale is most often small, designed to be unmolded for one person, but it can also be large, which makes an imposing presentation for two or more people. The nature of a timbale almost dictates that it be used as a first course presentation but it can do as a main lunch course. It is usually accompanied by a sauce of some sort. Here is a generic sort of timbale. I use broccoli, but you can substitute any other blanched, puréed, or finely chopped vegetable, fish, or meat. You may need as much as 2 1/2 cups of broccoli, depending on how finely you purée it, so be sure to cook enough.

1 tablespoon olive oil

2 cloves garlic, minced

4 tablespoons minced shallots

1 1/2 cups cooked, puréed broccoli

3 eggs, beaten

1/2 teaspoon salt and freshly ground pepper to taste

1 teaspoon curry powder

Heat oven to 325 degrees. Heat olive oil in a small sauté pan and cook the garlic and shallots until they are soft. Remove the contents of the pan to a small bowl and add the puréed broccoli, the beaten eggs, salt and freshly ground pepper, and curry powder.

Brush the insides of six timbale molds with olive oil. Fill molds to the top with the broccoli mixture and set them in a shallow baking pan. Pour boiling water to half-way up the sides of the molds and bake until set, about 25 minutes. The filling should shrink somewhat from the sides of the mold, and a sharp knife, when inserted into the mold, should come out clean. Run a knife around the edges of the molds and invert them onto individual serving plates. Spoon some béchamel sauce flavored with a little curry powder, or some fresh tomato sauce (see "Sauces") around the base of the timbale. Serve hot.

TIP: TO PURÉE BROCCOLI, SEPARATE THE FLORETS INTO SMALL PIECES AND PLACE THEM IN A POT OF RAPIDLY BOILING SALTED WATER. COOK THEM UNTIL THEY ARE TENDER, ABOUT 8 MINUTES. PLUNGE THEM IMMEDIATELY INTO A LARGE BOWL OF ICE WATER TO STOP THE COOKING AND SET THE COLOR. PURÉE THE COOLED FLORETS IN A BLENDER OR FOOD PROCESSOR. YOU CAN SUBSTITUTE ANY VEGETABLE PURÉE FOR THE BROCCOLI, USING A COMPATIBLE HERB OR SPICE IN PLACE OF THE CURRY POWDER. FOR EXAMPLE, A COMBINATION OF WILD AND DOMESTIC MUSHROOMS ACCENTED WITH THYME WOULD BE A GOOD COMBINATION. THE POSSIBILITIES ARE NUMEROUS, SO BE CREATIVE.

TURKISH OKRA AND TOMATO APPETIZER

YIELD: ABOUT 2 CUPS

3 cups fresh okra

2 or 3 medium tomatoes, peeled and cut into quarters

2 tablespoons olive oil

1 cup water, divided

1/2 teaspoon sugar

juice of 1/2 lemon

1/2 teaspoon salt

People who love to cook go to farmers' markets. They choose carefully, and go out of their way to buy the freshest, brightest produce. A perfect example of this is Natasha Flyer, whom we met while we were interviewing Bill West, who sells okra. She was overjoyed to find the reappearance of this much maligned vegetable in the market. To be perfectly honest, I had never liked okra. I didn't like the fuzzy skin, and I did not like the viscosity of the inside. But I'm open to new eating experiences. So I tried the recipe she shared with us as given to her by a Turkish friend, Luna Duenyas. The trick is not to cut into the okra, and not to overcook it. Just be sure to peel the skin at the stem end. This dish is usually part of an array of appetizers, called "meze" in Turkish, and it is eaten at room temperature.

Wash and peel the okra, trimming off the outer layer of skin at the stem end. Be careful not to cut through them. To peel the tomatoes, place them briefly in a small pot of boiling water. Plunge them into cold water, and the skins will slip right off. It is not necessary to remove the seeds for this recipe.

Heat oil in a small saucepan and add 1/2 cup water, sugar, and tomatoes. Cook for 3-4 minutes. Add the okra, lemon juice, the rest of the water, and salt. Cook over medium heat for 15 minutes. Remove from pot and serve at room temperature.

Tip: WHEN CHOOSING OKRA, LOOK FOR PODS WITH BRIGHT GREEN RIBS. PODS WITH BLACKISH LINES ARE NOT FRESH.

SOUPS AND SALADS

Soups and salads comprise the very heart of market cooking: thick tomato slices, golden beets, revitalizing stocks. The jaded palate is awakened by greens, pungent and crisp. Summer brings us variety, appetite encourages us to experiment, and the markets make all this available. These thick soups, basic stocks, and tingling salsas will excite the palate. Here is a new twist on potato soup, and an old twist with dill pickles. And best of all, the markets bring the riches to us.

AL'S DILL PICKLE SOUP

SERVES 6-8

1 tablespoon butter

1 medium onion, chopped

3 pickles from a jar of Vlasic (or similar) dill pickles, each about 4 inches

1/2 cup finely chopped carrots

1 1/2 cups peeled and diced potatoes

1 stalk celery, chopped fine

2 quarts chicken stock (see "Soups")

reserved pickle juice from 1 quart jar of dill pickles

salt and freshly ground pepper to taste

2 tablespoons flour

1 cup half and half or sour cream

No, your eyes have not deceived you. Al and Florence Kierczak's soup is made with the juices of a jar of "store-bought" pickles. Not a bad idea, if you think about it. We DO eat sweet and sour dishes, after all, and even just sour things, as in sauerbraten, so why not soup? This is based on a soup of Polish origin, and tastes great on a cold winter day.

Melt butter in a 3 quart pot and sauté onion until soft. Set aside. Grate pickles on a coarse grater or on the coarse disc of a food processor. Add grated pickles, chopped carrots, diced potatoes, chopped celery, chicken stock, and pickle juice to the sautéed onions. Cook until tender, about 30 minutes. Add salt and freshly ground pepper to taste.

Mix flour with 1/3 cup half and half or sour cream until it is dissolved. Add to soup, along with the remaining half and half or sour cream. Bring to a simmer and serve hot. As Al says, "Enjoy!"

APPLE, POTATO, AND CHEDDAR SOUP

SERVES 6

Good old apple pie with Cheddar cheese is transformed here into a tasty soup, thickened with potato and exalted by thyme. A crisp fall day, a walk in the woods, and a bowl of soup—or how about a rainy afternoon, a good book, a slothful snooze, and then a bowl of soup? In either case, this is a perfect choice. Use Granny Smith or Golden Delicious apples, or a combination of both. It's not necessary to peel them.

Heat olive oil in a large saucepan and add the apples, onion, fennel, celery, garlic, and dried thyme. Cook about 10 minutes, or until the solids are wilted and soft, but not brown. Add the white wine and scrape the bottom of the pan to remove any solids which may be sticking. Add the chicken stock and cubed potato and simmer another 20 minutes. Strain the soup and purée the solids, either in a food processor or a blender. Be careful not to over-process, or it will turn into a gluey mess. Return the solids and liquids to the pot and slowly add the grated cheese, fresh thyme, salt and pepper, heavy cream, and optional cayenne pepper. Cook until heated through, stirring frequently to keep it from sticking.

TIP: THIS SOUP IS GOOD GARNISHED WITH CROUTONS, CUBES OF FRESH APPLE, AND A SPRINKLING OF THYME LEAVES. YOU MAY ALSO SUBSTITUTE YOGURT FOR THE HEAVY CREAM.

3 tablespoons olive oil

4 apples, cored and cut into 1-inch cubes (Granny Smith or Golden Delicious)

1/2 cup diced onion

1/2 cup diced fresh fennel

1/2 cup diced celery

1 clove garlic, minced or pressed

3/4 teaspoon dried thyme

1/3 cup white wine

6 cups chicken stock

1 large potato, peeled and cut into 1 inch cubes

4 1/2 cups grated sharp Cheddar cheese

1 teaspoon fresh thyme leaves

salt and freshly ground pepper to taste

1/2 cup heavy cream

pinch of cayenne pepper (optional)

ARUGULA AND GOLDEN BEET
SALAD WITH GOAT CHEESE

═══════ SERVES 6 ═══════

2 bunches arugula

2 cups mesclun

3 or 4 medium size golden beets

1/4 cup mustard vinaigrette (see Vinaigrette Mother in "Embellishments")

1/2 cup roasted pecans (see "Basics"), salted

4 ounces goat cheese, sliced or crumbled

How did we live without arugula? It appeared on the food scene some years ago and quickly became the salad green of choice. Its slightly bitter yet nutty flavor provides a fine background for tangy mustard vinaigrette and roasted pecans. Golden beets are less earthy tasting than the traditional red ones, and are beautiful against the deep green of the leafy arugula. Mesclun is a mixture of baby greens. Both arugula and mesclun are available at the outdoor Farmers' Market during the summer, but you can also find them at Zingerman's Practical Produce at Kerrytown or the People's Food Co-op during the winter. You may use hazelnuts or walnuts instead of pecans, but be sure to roast them to develop their full flavor.

Cut off and discard long stems of the arugula and soak leaves in a large bowl of cold water. Drain and dry leaves in a salad spinner or between sheets of paper toweling.

Scrub beets and remove stem ends. In a pot large enough to hold them, cover them with water and bring water to a boil. Lower heat, cover, and cook until beets are tender, about 30 minutes. Drain beets and place them in a large bowl of cold water. The skins should slip off easily. Cut them into 1/4 inch slices, then cut the slices in half. Reserve.

Combine washed and dried arugula, mesclun, and beets in a large bowl, and toss lightly with mustard vinaigrette. Divide salad among 6 chilled plates and garnish with the roasted pecans and goat cheese.

TIP: SPRINKLE A LITTLE POP-CORN SALT ON THE PECANS JUST AFTER ROASTING THEM, WHILE THEY ARE STILL HOT.

ASPARAGUS SOUP

SERVES 6-8

Early spring days bring out the best of the cook in me. After winter meals of gutsy stews and hearty soups, and even though the nights may still be a bit snappy and cool, I yearn for something green and smelling of spring. What fills the bill better than asparagus soup? Of course, when you're making soup, it doesn't matter whether you like your asparagus thin or thick, but it is a luxurious feeling to be able to take advantage of the Farmers' Market and choose individual spears. This soup freezes very well.

Wash asparagus and cut off the woody ends. Trim stalks into 1 inch pieces, reserving 16 tips. Heat butter and olive oil in a 6-8 quart stock pot. Over low heat, sauté the leeks, onions, and garlic until soft, but not brown. Add the curry powder and continue to cook for another minute. Add the chicken stock, potato, and cut asparagus to the stock pot, and cook for 25-30 minutes, or until the asparagus is tender. While soup is cooking, blanch the asparagus tips by cooking them in 1 quart of boiling water for 3 minutes. When they are cooked but still crisp, remove them with a slotted spoon and plunge them into a bowl of very cold water. This will set their color. When they are cool, drain and dry them. If not using immediately, store in a plastic bag in refrigerator. To return to the soup: using a slotted spoon or a strainer, transfer solids from the pot to a food processor or blender. Purée until smooth. Return purée to the liquids in the stock pot and add the cream. Add salt and pepper. Taste and adjust seasonings, if necessary. Serve soup hot or cold, garnished with the reserved asparagus tips and chopped chives or scallions.

3-4 pounds asparagus

3 tablespoons olive oil

1 tablespoon butter

1 leek, white part only, cleaned and thinly sliced

1 medium onion, chopped

2 or 3 cloves garlic, minced or pressed

1 teaspoon curry powder

6-7 cups chicken stock

1 medium potato, diced

2/3 cup heavy cream or half and half

1 teaspoon salt or to taste

freshly ground black pepper to taste

4 tablespoons chopped chives or scallions

CATHERINE RESKE'S POTATO LEEK SOUP

SERVES 6-8

4 ounces butter or olive oil

5 cups chopped leeks, white and light green parts only

1 medium onion, chopped

2 quarts chicken stock or water

4 cups roughly chopped peeled potatoes

2 stalks celery, chopped

1 medium carrot, peeled and cut into rough dice

2 cups chopped cabbage (optional)

salt and freshly ground pepper to taste

2 tablespoons chopped fresh dill or 1 teaspoon dried dill or to taste

It is amazing to see how many variations of potato leek soup there are. Each variation seems to have been tailored to fit the palate of the creator. In this case, cabbage and carrots are added to the basic ingredients, enhancing the soup much as individual instruments blend into a symphony, adding indefinable characteristics to the whole.

Heady language for a soup, you say? Try it. You'll see what I mean.

Melt butter in a 2 quart saucepan and sauté chopped leeks and onion over low heat until they are soft, but not brown. Set aside.

Bring chicken stock or water to a simmer and add the potatoes, celery, carrot, and cabbage. Simmer for 20 minutes. Add the sautéed leek mixture and simmer another 10 minutes. Purée the soup in a blender or food processor. Be careful not to over-process, or it will turn gluey. Add fresh or dried dill, and serve with a hearty rye or pumpernickel bread.

CHICKEN STOCK

YIELD: ABOUT 6 CUPS

If you prefer a browner stock, brown the chicken parts and the vegetables in a 400 degree oven before proceeding with the recipe. You may also include the bones and meat from cooked poultry, but remember that the flavorings you used to make the original recipe will accent the final stock. You may want to double this recipe, since it freezes very well.

Place all of the ingredients except the thyme and rosemary in a 5 quart pot and bring to a boil. Lower heat and simmer partially covered, for 2 hours. Skim off any foam which rises to the surface and discard. Add the thyme and rosemary about 1/2 hour before stock is done. Cool stock to room temperature and strain through a fine sieve or cheesecloth. Chill in refrigerator and remove fat which has congealed on the surface. Freeze if not using within 2 days.

3 pounds chicken pieces (backs, necks, trimmings)

3 quarts water

2 carrots, peeled, chopped

2 stalks celery, leaves included, chopped

1 large onion, cut in half

1 or 2 medium turnips, peeled and cut into quarters

6-8 whole peppercorns

1 tablespoon salt

2 bay leaves

2 or 3 sprigs each of fresh thyme and rosemary

FISH STOCK

5 pounds fish frames, including heads, skins, and bones

1 large onion, outer skin removed

2 or 3 large carrots, peeled and cut into chunks

2 ribs celery, leaves and all, cleaned and cut into chunks

1 leek, green and white parts, cleaned and cut into chunks

5 bay leaves

4 or 5 peppercorns

1 teaspoon salt

1 large frond of fennel (optional)

"Be prepared," says the old Scout motto. So here is a fish stock that freezes very well, and when you need it, there it is. It can be used as a base for fish sauces, chowders, and fish soups. The heads of the fish are important in producing a gelatin, which adds a fine dimension to the stock. When wine is added to fish stock, the result is referred to as a "fumet."

Simmer the five pounds of fish heads, bones, and skins in water to cover, along with the onion, carrots, celery, and leek, all cut into chunks. Add bay leaves, peppercorns, and salt. Simmer for 1-2 hours, discarding any foamy scum that rises to the surface. Strain through cheesecloth and reserve for future use in 2 cup containers. Freezes well.

KOHLRABI SOUP

YIELD: 6-8 SERVINGS

Kohlrabi, that vegetable that looks as if it came from outer space, is really quite tasty. Eaten raw, it is crisp and juicy. It is a member of a family of vegetables called "oleraceae" (often called "coles") which includes cauliflower, kale and broccoli, among others. Kohlrabi's most common color is light green, although it is also sometimes a pale violet shade. Here is another Al and Florence Kierczak soup recipe. (See Al's Sauerkraut Soup.)

Combine all of the ingredients except the cream in a 4 or 5 quart pot. Cook until tender. Add cream. Serve hot.

Tip: WE PURÉED THIS SOUP AND LIKED IT THAT WAY, TOO.

**3 quarts beef stock
(see "Boiled Beef Dinner")**

1 cup chopped, peeled kohlrabi

1 1/2 cups diced new potatoes, skin on

1 medium onion, diced

1 small carrot, peeled and chopped

1 cup chopped cabbage

1/2 cup chopped fresh basil

1 clove garlic, minced

salt and freshly ground pepper to taste

1 cup cream, milk, or sour cream

MESCLUN SALAD

4 cups mesclun

1 cup bite-size romaine lettuce pieces

1 cup bite-size leaf lettuce pieces

1/2 cup peeled and diced jicama (1/2 inch dice)

1/2 peeled and diced avocado (1/2 inch dice)

8 kumquats, cut into thin rounds, seeds removed

1/2 cup mustard vinaigrette (see "Embellishments")

1/2 cup roasted walnut halves (see "Basics")

The fresh baby greens in a mesclun salad, though tender and subtle, can also be assertive and crunchy. Pale whitish-green frisée, vibrant raddichio, nutty emerald arugula, and young spinach are some of the components of the washed and dried mesclun salad available at the Farmers' Market and at almost all of the produce suppliers in the Kerrytown area. Mesclun can be eaten as is, or glorified with a myriad of ingredients: goat cheese, avocado, jicama, or roasted pecans, for example. You can also nestle grilled quail, or poached chicken breast, or cold roast lamb, or plain old deviled eggs atop of a mound of crisp mesclun, drizzle a fragrant vinaigrette over all, and create a great meal.

Combine all of the ingredients except the toasted walnuts. Distribute among 6 chilled plates and top with roasted walnut halves.

PLUM SALSA

This spicy salsa is best made with firm, dark-skinned plums. It can be served hot or at room temperature, and tastes just right when served with a simple fish fillet or a smoky piece of grilled beef. Be sure to roast the cumin seeds before you grind them to release their full flavor (see "Basics").

Prepare the plums by first cutting around the seed. Use a sharp knife and dice the plums into approximately 1/2 inch cubes. Repeat this procedure with the mango. Try to keep the size of all the cut produce approximately the same, except for the purple onion, which should be chopped into a smaller dice. Combine all of the diced fruits and vegetables as you cut them. Peel the cucumber and cut it into halves, the long way. Scoop out the seeds with a spoon, and lay the cut side of each half down on a wooden board. Cut each half into long strips. Dice the strips into 1/2 inch cubes. Add the diced red pepper. The garlic may be cut into fine dice with a sharp knife, or, if you wish, put through a garlic press. If the garlic has a bright green center, remove it before you dice or press it. (This little beginning shoot may make your salsa bitter.) Add the jalapeño pepper. To chop the fresh coriander leaves, first remove the stems, then make a tight bunch of the leaves. Use a sharp knife and chop the leaves as finely as you can. Alternatively, you can use a scissors to cut the leaves. Add the cayenne, cumin seed, salt, and rice vinegar. Mix all of these ingredients thoroughly. The salsa should sit for at least an hour before you serve it.

TIP: YOU CAN MAKE THIS SALSA AS LONG AS ONE DAY AHEAD. IT WILL KEEP FOR SEVERAL DAYS IN THE REFRIGERATOR. AN AVOCADO, PEELED, SEEDED, AND DICED, MAY BE ADDED JUST BEFORE YOU SERVE THE SALSA.

2 cups diced firm, unpeeled, dark-skinned, yellow flesh plums

1 cup diced mango

1/2 cup chopped purple onion

1 cup peeled and diced cucumber (seeds removed)

1/2 cup diced red pepper

2 cloves garlic, finely diced

1 teaspoon chopped fresh jalapeño pepper

1/3 cup chopped fresh cilantro leaves

1/2 teaspoon cayenne pepper

1 teaspoon roasted ground cumin seed

1/2 teaspoon salt

1/4 cup rice vinegar

AL'S SAUERKRAUT SOUP

═══ SERVES 6-8 ═══

2 quarts water

1/2 quart rinsed sauerkraut

1 tablespoon olive oil

1 medium onion, chopped

1 cup diced, peeled potatoes

1/2 carrot, peeled and finely diced

1 10 ounce can cream of mushroom soup, undiluted

4 strips bacon, fried crisp, then crumbled (fat reserved)

3 tablespoons flour

Forget your dieting, forget your cholesterol count, forget avoiding commercially prepared ingredients. This is a GOOD soup. The little bit of bacon fat and the canned cream of mushroom soup make this soup what it is. So don't substitute. But if you really, really must eliminate all animal fat from your diet, see the tip at the end of the recipe.

Cook sauerkraut in water for 30 minutes. Reserve. Heat olive oil in a small sauté pan and cook the chopped onion until it is soft. Add sautéed onion, potatoes, carrot, cream of mushroom soup, and crumbled bacon to the cooked sauerkraut. Simmer another 30 minutes. Add flour to the reserved bacon fat, and fry until brown. Add 1 cup of hot soup to the browned fat in the pan and stir to emulsify. Return this browned flour mixture to the soup in the pot, and stir well to thicken. Simmer, stirring with a wooden spoon occasionally, for another 20-30 minutes. Serve hot. Al and Florence say, "Bon Appétit!"

TIP: YOU CAN REPLACE THE BACON WITH A FEW DROPS OF BOTTLED HICKORY "SMOKE".

STRAWBERRY SOUP

You went to the market and couldn't resist buying that flat of strawberries. So aromatic, so perfectly shaped, so ruby-red. You waited one day before doing anything with them, and here they are, a little bruised looking, blurry around the edges, but still heady with flavor, their seductive perfume almost overwhelming. Too late for tarts, and you don't feel like making jam. What to do? Make soup! Serve it as a first course, or as a dessert—it doesn't matter. The ambrosian strawberry flavor is still there in all its glory.

Place strawberries in the bowl of a food processor and purée until smooth. Add all of the remaining ingredients and process briefly. Refrigerate until serving. Ladle into soup bowls and garnish with sliced strawberries and a sprig of basil or mint.

4 cups cleaned, hulled strawberries

1/3 cup orange juice

1 1/2 cups lowfat buttermilk

1 cup low fat vanilla flavored yogurt

3 teaspoons sugar

1/4 teaspoon ground nutmeg

1/2 teaspoon roasted ground fennel seed (see "Basics")

reserved strawberries for garnish

sprigs of fresh basil or mint (optional)

TOMATO, ORANGE, AND VIDALIA ONION SALAD

═══ SERVES 6 ═══

4 large, ripe, red tomatoes

2 navel oranges, peeled

2 Vidalia onions, peeled

8-10 black oil-cured olives, pitted, chopped

1/4 cup vinaigrette (see "Embellishments")

2 tablespoons chopped fresh parsley

There is simply nothing like the taste of a summer tomato, warm from the sun, heavy in the hand. Although this salad proves the point, it will still taste pretty good in the winter, when navel oranges are at their best and Vidalia onions are still in the market. It's an attractive addition to a buffet table, and with a few anchovy fillets, some goat cheese, and rye bread it makes a luscious lunch.

Slice tomatoes, oranges, and Vidalia onions into 1/4 inch slices. Arrange slices in an alternating pattern on a serving platter large enough to hold them. Sprinkle chopped olives on top. At least an hour before serving, pour the vinaigrette over the top and sprinkle with chopped parsley.

TIP: TO BRING OUT THE FULL FLAVOR OF THE TOMATOES, SERVE THIS AT ROOM TEMPERATURE.

TOMATO AND GARLIC SOUP

SERVES 6-8

The aroma of this soup drifts from the windows of homes in the Perigord region of France, where it is a staple of the area. They call it "Tourain." The pungency and sweetness of fresh tomatoes combined with garlic, eggs, and vinegar results in a simple, yet elegant soup. The French use goose fat, but I have substituted olive oil, which does change the taste a bit. If you are lucky enough to have goose or chicken or even duck fat, by all means use it, especially if your cholesterol count can take it. There's nothing to equal their flavor and the extra dimension they add to the soup.

Using a heavy 6 or 8 quart pot, over medium heat, sauté the garlic and onions in the olive oil. When they are soft but not brown, add the flour, immediately stirring it with a wooden spoon. Heat another minute or two. Chop the peeled, seeded tomatoes and add them to the mixture.

Add the water or chicken stock. Simmer the soup for 30 minutes over low heat. Add salt and freshly ground pepper to taste.

Carefully transfer the contents of the pot, a little at a time, to a food processor and purée until smooth. Mix beaten eggs, vinegar, and parsley together. Add some of the warm puréed soup to the egg mixture. Return the soup/egg mixture to the pot, and heat gently. Taste for seasoning, and adjust if necessary. Pour into individual soup bowls, top each with a piece of rye toast, and serve hot.

10 cloves garlic, peeled

3 medium onions, thinly sliced

3 tablespoons olive oil (or rendered goose, chicken, or duck fat (see "Basics")

3 tablespoons flour

5 cups Roma tomatoes, peeled and seeds squeezed out (see "Basics")

1 cup water or chicken stock

3 eggs, room temperature, beaten

2 teaspoons red wine vinegar

4 tablespoons chopped flat-leafed parsley

6-8 pieces thick rye bread, toasted and rubbed with garlic

VEGETABLE STOCK

2 medium onions, peeled and
coarsely chopped

1 whole leek, white and green
parts, cleaned and coarsely
chopped

2 medium size carrots,
peeled and coarsely chopped

4 celery stalks, including leaves,
roughly diced

1 medium tomato,
cut into quarters

2 or 3 sprigs of parsley

1 small turnip, peeled and cut
into quarters

1/2 medium cabbage,
coarsely chopped

1 teaspoon salt

4 or 5 peppercorns

3 or 4 bay leaves, crumbled

3 quarts water

For those recipes that mandate keeping everything vegetarian, here is a full-flavored stock. You may add or subtract any vegetables you like. I personally find that turnips and cabbage are absolutely necessary, for they contribute a dimension of flavor that no other vegetables can.

Place all of the above ingredients in a 4 or 5 quart pot and bring to a boil. Place a lid slightly ajar on the pot, lower heat, and simmer for 1 1/2 to 2 hrs. Check liquid in the pot occasionally, and add more water to maintain about 3 quarts of stock. Drain contents of pot through cheesecloth, or a fine strainer. Taste for seasonings, and adjust if necessary. Cool the stock. Store in refrigerator or freezer.

TIP: THE COOKED VEGETABLES WILL YIELD MOST OF THEIR FLAVOR TO THE STOCK, BUT NEVERTHELESS MAKE A TASTY, FAT–FREE SNACK WHEN COUPLED WITH DIJON MUSTARD OR HORSERADISH.

ENTRÉES

American menus sometimes seem confusing to foreign visitors.
An entrée in Europe is a course usually served between the fish
and the main course in a formal dinner. To Americans, it is the
main course, even if the dinner is not formal, and that is what it
means here. From a simple boiled beef dinner to trendy squash
enchiladas, these recipes make use of the fresh produce and fine
products of the Ann Arbor Farmers' Market and the Kerrytown
area food shops. Spinach pie, herb-stuffed pork loin, smoked
salmon cakes, and root vegetable risotto are among the recipes
in this chapter.

BOILED BEEF DINNER

cheesecloth

3 pounds beef chuck or beef
brisket, bones optional

3 medium turnips, peeled,
cut in half

2 carrots, peeled, cut in half

1 medium onion, peeled,
cut in half

1/2 medium cabbage, trimmed,
cut into chunks

8 small potatoes (or four large),
peeled, left whole (or cut in half)

8 peppercorns

2 teaspoons salt

4 bay leaves

The fragrant broth produced by this recipe is one of those diet freebies of the culinary world. So aromatic, so satisfying, so simple. I've tried eliminating one or another of the ingredients, or substituting other vegetables for the basic ones in the recipe, but frankly, it is not quite the same. Still delicious, but different. I recommend that you follow the recipe first, and then experiment if you like. This is a real "hands across the front door" recipe between the indoor and outdoor markets. Purchase either beef brisket or chuck roast with or without the bone at Bob Sparrow's meat market. Add a marrow bone if that's to your taste. The only vegetables I would not replace in this recipe are the turnips and cabbage. They seem to be the soul of the soup.

Rinse cheesecloth in cold water and wrap meat and optional bones in it, tying the ends of the cloth firmly together. Place all of the ingredients in an 8 quart stock pot. Cover with water, and bring mixture to a boil over high heat. Turn heat down to a simmer and cook until meat is tender, about 2 hours. Skim off any scum that rises to the surface as the stock is cooking. Cool stock and remove meat. Unwrap the meat and bones and trim off any cartilage or fat. Cut meat into portion sizes and return it to the pot. When you are ready to serve the soup, warm the bowls and ladle portions of each vegetable and meat into the warm bowls. Serve with horseradish, various mustards, and a substantial rye or pumpernickel bread.

TIP: WRAPPING THE MEAT IN CHEESECLOTH AS IT COOKS WILL KEEP ANY BITS OF FAT FROM DISLODGING AND THEREBY IMPROVE THE CLARITY OF THE SOUP. RINSING THE CHEESECLOTH IN COLD WATER BEFORE USING WILL GET RID OF ANY SIZING TASTE.

CHICKEN STRUDEL

SERVES 8-10

The excellent chicken breasts from Sparrow Meat help make this presentation as delicious as it is elegant. One of the good things about this recipe is that it can be prepared in advance and then popped into the oven whenever you need it. When made with a brioche dough, or a puff pastry dough, this loaf is called a "coulibiac," which is a Russian term for a dish that usually includes a melange of rice, vegetables, and usually salmon encased in dough. Because we are using a filo dough, we are calling it a "strudel." By any name, it is really quite spectacular.

Sauté chopped leek and 1/2 tablespoon minced garlic in 1 tablespoon olive oil. Press out all of the water from the steamed spinach using a fine sieve. Place spinach, with the sautéed leek and garlic in a food processor, and while it is on, add 3 of the egg whites, 1/2 teaspoon salt, pepper, and the nutmeg. Process until it is well combined. Keep spinach mixture chilled while proceeding with the recipe. Cut the chicken breast into one inch pieces, and process in food processor until smooth. With the machine on, add the remaining egg whites, divided, and the 1/2 cup cream in a slow stream. Add 1 teaspoon salt, freshly ground pepper, the rest of the puréed garlic, and 2 tablespoons of the chopped fresh dill or tarragon. Process briefly. Chill. Combine the rice with the remaining chopped fresh dill or tarragon, 1 teaspoon roasted cumin seeds, and the béchamel sauce. Lay four sheets of filo dough on a sheet of parchment paper, or waxed paper, brushing melted butter between each sheet, and on top of the fourth layer. Construct the strudels, layering the ingredients along the lower third of the filo in the following manner:

Mound half of the spinach mousse along the bottom of the rectangle, leaving a 2 inch edge all around. Top this with pieces of roasted pepper, smooth side down. Cover this with a layer of half of the chicken mousse, and finally, half of the turmeric rice. Fold the sides of the filo dough inward, and then roll the filled strudel away from you, enclosing all of the ingredients. Use the parchment or waxed paper to help you roll up the strudel. Be careful not to push too hard, as the layers will slide. Place on the baking sheet with the seam on the bottom. Repeat these instructions to make a second strudel. Chill for at least one hour. Brush the top of the strudel with melted butter, or spray it with a vegetable oil. Heat oven to 350 degrees and bake for 45 minutes, or until the dough is a golden brown. Cool and store in refrigerator or at room temperature for a few hours to allow all of the ingredients to "set". Slice into individual portions, and serve as a first course. It can be served chilled but is better warm or at room temperature.

1 cleaned leek, chopped

5 tablespoons minced garlic, divided

2 tablespoons olive oil, divided

3 pounds fresh spinach, washed, tough stems removed, steamed

5 egg whites

1/2 teaspoon salt and freshly ground pepper to taste

1/4 teaspoon ground nutmeg

1 1/2 pounds boneless raw chicken breast

1/2 cup heavy cream

1 teaspoon salt and freshly ground pepper to taste

1 cup chopped fresh dill or tarragon, divided

1/4 cup olive oil

1 teaspoon salt, and freshly ground pepper to taste

2 cups rice cooked with 1 teaspoon turmeric powder

1 teaspoon roasted cumin seeds (see "Basics")

1 cup béchamel sauce (see "Sauces")

3 or 4 roasted red peppers (see "Basics") cut into lengthwise quarters

1/2 cup melted butter

1 package thawed filo dough

DUCK BREAST SEARED WITH JUNIPER BERRIES AND GARLIC

SERVES 6

This elegant entrée can be partially prepared well in advance, then finished off without too much last minute attention. Whole duck breasts are available from from Bob Sparrow's market at Kerrytown (remove and save the skin). Serve with a classical mixture of puréed turnips and potatoes, and Juniper Port Wine Sauce, and invite your favorite friends to enjoy this seemingly complicated meal. Allow at least 1 hour to marinate the breasts, or marinate them overnight for convenience. Pulverize the juniper berries by placing them in a plastic bag and crushing them with the edge of a small heavy pot, or with a rolling pin. If you have a small spice grinder, use that, but be sure not to grind them too fine, as their flavor will overpower the duck.

1 tablespoon chopped fresh thyme

1 tablespoon commercially dried coarsely pulverized juniper berries

3 cloves garlic, pressed or minced

2 tablespoons olive oil

3 whole duck breasts, cut in half

salt and freshly ground pepper to taste

2 tablespoons vegetable oil

Combine the chopped thyme, juniper berries, and garlic with the olive oil. Marinate duck pieces in the oil/herb mixture for at least one hour at room temperature. (You may also do this one day ahead, refrigerated.) Heat oven to 450 degrees. Remove the duck breasts from the marinade and salt and pepper them. In a heavy pan heat the vegetable oil until it smokes. Sear the duck breasts on both sides, about one minute on each side. Strain and reserve cooking juices. (You may do this step a few hours ahead, but if you do, bring them to room temperature before cooking.) Place breasts on a heatproof shallow pan and cook them in a hot oven about 5 minutes. The meat should give a little when you press on it, and it will continue to cook after you remove it from the oven. Duck breast is usually served quite rare. Allow the meat to rest a few minutes before slicing into long thin slices diagonally. You should get about 5 slices per portion. Serve on a heated plate with Juniper Port Wine Sauce (see "Sauces") and Potato-Turnip Purée (see "Side Dishes").

TIP: FOR A REAL TREAT (NOT FOR THOSE WHO NEED TO WATCH THEIR FAT INTAKE), CUT UP THE DUCK SKIN INTO SMALL SQUARES AND ROAST THEM ON A SHEET PAN IN A 350 DEGREE OVEN UNTIL THE FAT IS RENDERED AND THE SQUARES ARE CRISP. USE THESE LITTLE BITS OF CHOLESTEROL-LADEN HEAVEN TO GARNISH A SPINACH SALAD OR AN OMELET.

EGGPLANT "BIRDS"

SERVES 4

There are tiny eggplants, large eggplants, slender eggplants, white eggplants, oval, round and pear-shaped eggplants. They vary slightly in taste, and their sizes and shapes offer a range of cooking techniques. For this recipe, we are using the familiar pear-shaped, dark purple-skinned one. Choose a firm eggplant that returns to its shape when you press it lightly and that has a tight skin free of any mold. This dish is good with chicken or fish, or simply by itself as a light lunch. I call them "birds" because when the slices are rolled up they resemble plump little fowl.

Do not peel the eggplant before slicing. Heat oven to 350 degrees.

Sprinkle salt on eggplant slices, and set them to drain in a colander. After about 15 minutes, they will give off a lot of moisture. Blot slices with a paper towel, and brush or spray each one with olive oil. Rub with minced garlic and sprinkle roasted, ground cumin on each slice. Arrange slices on an oiled baking sheet and bake for 15 minutes, turning once. When the slices are limp and light brown, remove them from the pan. While eggplant slices are roasting, cut zucchini into thin 1/4 inch rounds. Cut roasted red peppers into small rectangles about 1 inch by 2 1/2 inches.

To assemble the "birds," lay a slice of eggplant on a flat surface, long side perpendicular to the edge of the counter. Place 1 teaspoon of grated cheese in a pile on the center of the slice. Lay a rectangle of roasted red pepper on top, followed by more cheese. Place 1 or 2 slices of zucchini on top of this pile, then more cheese. Working from the bottom up, roll the eggplant firmly around the filling. Place the completed roll seam side down in an oiled gratin dish, and proceed in the same way with the rest of the slices. When all of the eggplant slices have been filled, spray or brush olive oil over them, and sprinkle any remaining cheese on top. Cover loosely with aluminum foil and bake in 350 oven for 30 minutes, or until eggplant is soft. (You can refrigerate prepared "birds" and bake them any time in the next two days.)

TIP: A SLICE OF PARTIALLY COOKED POTATO OR A TEASPOON OR SO OF CHOPPED BLACK OLIVES MAKES AN INTERESTING ADDITION TO THE FILLING.

TIP: THIN SLICES OF ALREADY COOKED "BIRDS" FANNED OUT ON A PLATE MAKE AN ATTRACTIVE, RELATIVELY LOW FAT, SERENDIPITOUS NIBBLE.

2 eggplants, cut into 1/4 inch slices, sliced from blossom end to wide end

1 teaspoon salt

2 tablespoons olive oil or olive oil spray

2 cloves garlic, minced or pressed

2 tablespoons roasted, ground cumin seed (see "Basics")

2 zucchini, about 7 inches long

2 large red peppers, roasted and peeled (see "Basics")

3/4 cup (or more to taste) grated Parmesan Reggiano cheese

more olive oil spray

SWORDFISH WITH FOUR PEPPERS

SERVES 6

6 pieces swordfish steak, 6 ounces each

3 tablespoons olive oil

1/4 cup each black, pink, and white peppercorns

2 large shallots, minced

1 tablespoon butter

3 cups red wine (Beaujolais type)

3 tablespoons meat glaze (optional)

2 cups fish stock (see "Soups")

1/4 cup heavy cream

1/4 cup green peppercorns, pickled, not dried

This is a dish for those who like pepper, without a doubt. The green peppercorns are soft and tender, and are, therefore, incorporated into the dish at the end. Meat glaze is a preparation found in many commercial and some home kitchens. You may substitute 1 cup of beef stock reduced to 3 tablespoons. This dish goes very well with Julienne of Vegetables (see "Side Dishes").

Rub fish steaks on both sides with olive oil. Coarsely grind the black, white, and pink peppercorns, and sprinkle over fish on both sides. Allow to marinate for at least 1 hour and as long as 3 hours. (If desired, the fish may be coated with the olive oil and placed in refrigerator overnight in a glass or porcelain dish. The peppercorns should not be added too long before cooking—three hours maximum.) Sauté the minced shallots in 1 tablespoon of butter until soft. Pour in the 3 cups of red wine and simmer until reduced by one third. Add the optional meat glaze. Strain and reserve the sauce in a 1 quart pot.

Heat a platter for the fish. Heat a large sauté pan until very hot, then add fish. You may need more than one pan because it is important not to crowd the pieces of fish together. If more oil is needed, add as necessary. Turn fish steaks after 5 minutes, and cook another 2 minutes. Remove to the warm platter and keep warm.

Deglaze the sauté pan with 1-2 cups of fish stock, scraping the residue from the bottom of the pan. When liquid is reduced by half, add the 1/4 cup heavy cream. Strain the mixture into the reserved red wine sauce. Taste for seasonings, adding salt if necessary. If sauce is too thin, you may thicken it by mixing 2 tablespoons arrowroot in 1/4 cup wine and adding it to sauce just as it reaches a boil. Do not cook it too long, or the sauce will break apart . You may also thicken it with 2 tablespoons of cornstarch dissolved in 1/2 cup wine, and added to the rest of the sauce as it cooks. Another method for thickening is to knead equal parts butter and flour together and whisk into simmering sauce. Strain sauce into a small pot, add the green pickled peppercorns, and keep warm. Spoon a little over fish just before serving, and pass the rest.

Tip: You can use grouper or even salmon fillets in place of the swordfish. Indeed, substitute any fish you like, but the more assertive the flavor the better, because the red wine sauce and the peppercorns, needless to say, are powerful components of the dish.

GNOCCHI

═ SERVES 4-6 ═

Gnocchi are little oval shapes made of various combinations of potatoes and flour, or ricotta cheese, with or without spinach, and flour, or semolina. They may be boiled and baked, or simply boiled and served with one of a variety of sauces. Eating gnocchi made with fresh potatoes is an experience that defies description. Don't expect to eat much else. They will fill you with such satisfaction that the only other thing you might want to eat is more of the same. Since there are so few ingredients in this recipe, each one matters a lot, and fresh potatoes from the outdoor Farmers' Market make this dish a very special treat.

3 pounds large, whole Russet-type potatoes, unpeeled

approximately 2 cups all purpose flour

1 teaspoon salt

4 ounces butter, melted and clarified (see "Basics")

2 cups freshly grated Parmesan Reggiano cheese

salt and freshly ground pepper to taste

Boil washed, unpeeled potatoes in a large amount of unsalted water. Leaving the potatoes unpeeled protects them against being water-logged, so less flour is need in the dough. When potatoes are tender, remove them from the pot with a slotted spoon and peel them. Put them through a potato ricer and while they are still hot, place them in a pile on a wooden board or counter that you have sprinkled with some of the flour. Mix in most of the flour at once, reserving about 1/4 cup to add to the mixture, should you require it. Knead the dough until it is smooth and malleable. Cut dough into sections, and roll each section into a "rope" about 1/2 inch in diameter. Cut the ropes into 1/2 inch to 3/4 inch sections. Using a fork with long tines, place a nugget of dough in the hollow at the base of the tines. (The fork should be held eating side up.) Pressing gently with the palm of your hand, roll the gnocchi toward the tip of the tines and allow it to drop onto the board. (This is not as difficult to do as it sounds.) This will form a grooved oval shape. The shape ensures even cooking, and the grooves will catch and hold any sauce you choose to use. While the dough is being formed, boil a very large quantity (at least 6 quarts) of water with a teaspoon of salt. Drop about a third of the gnocchi into the water at one time. As soon as they float to the surface, remove them with a slotted spoon. Drain them thoroughly and transfer them to a heated shallow bowl. (Make sure to drain any water which may have dripped into the bowl.) Pour a little melted butter or sauce over them as you transfer them to the bowl. Continue this step until all of the gnocchi are cooked. (When all of the gnocchi are cooked, pour the rest of the melted butter over them, add salt and pepper to taste, then the grated Parmesan cheese. Serve at once, passing more grated cheese if desired.

Tip: Be sure to use a good quality Parmesan. You can choose to serve the gnocchi with a pesto sauce, or with a gorgonzola sauce (see "Sauces").

Tip: You can incorporate some gorgonzola cheese into the ropes of dough before you roll out the gnocchi shapes.

HARVEST FRITTATA

1 tablespoon olive oil, divided

1 medium onion, diced

4 cloves garlic, minced or pressed

1 roasted medium pimiento or red pepper, julienned (see "Basics")

2 medium zucchini, julienned

1 medium Portobello mushroom, julienned

1 cup cooked corn

4 tablespoons capers

1 teaspoon salt

1/2 teaspoon freshly ground pepper

1 tablespoon roasted ground cumin seed (see "Basics")

1 tablespoon dried oregano

1 teaspoon dried thyme

8 ounces cottage cheese, whipped

12 large eggs, beaten

1/2 cup milk

8 ounces cream cheese, room temperature

1 cup grated or shredded Cheddar cheese

1 cup grated Parmesan cheese

3 cups cooked pasta, such as fettucine, spaghetti, or linguine

Don't get excited when you see that there are a dozen eggs in this recipe. That's only one and a half per person, and this is a lunch or supper recipe. This frittata is a little unusual in that it uses pasta as one of its ingredients, and is loaded with all the wonderful fresh vegetables we try to eat at the end of summer because we know that they will soon be gone. Who doesn't like pasta?

Heat oven to 350 degrees, and use some of the olive oil to grease a large 12 cup soufflé dish, or a 10 inch springform pan.

Heat remaining oil in a large sauté pan and cook the onion and garlic until they are soft. Add the pimiento, zucchini, Portobello mushroom, and corn, and cook another 10 minutes. Add the capers, salt, pepper, cumin, oregano, and thyme and cook another minute to blend the flavors. Set aside and proceed with the rest of the recipe.

Place the cottage cheese in the bowl of a food processor and whip until smooth. Add the eggs and blend. Add the milk and cream cheese and blend again until the mixture is smooth. Pour the mixture into a large bowl and add the Cheddar and Parmesan cheeses and the cooked vegetables and pasta. Taste for seasonings, and adjust, if necessary.

Pour mixture into the soufflé dish or springform pan and bake about 45-50 minutes, or until it is set. Let the cooked frittata sit for 10 minutes before removing sides of springform pan. This will help it keep its shape better. If you have made this in a soufflé dish, scoop out the portions. If you have made it in a springform pan, cut it into wedges. Serve with Fresh Tomato Sauce (see "Sauces") or Olive Anchovy Paste (see "Embellishments").

HERBED STUFFED PORK LOIN

═══ SERVES 6 ═══

This dish is made outstanding by its use of fennel seed, prunes, and apricots. The roasted and ground fennel seed is combined with chopped garlic, prunes, and dried apricots to form a filling for the pork loin. The loin is then rolled in more ground fennel seed, seared over high heat, and roasted. The cooked roast is cooled, then sliced, if it is to be served at room temperature within a few hours. (I like it best this way.) It also may be prepared a day in advance, but should be brought to room temperature before serving to bring out the full flavor of the ingredients. You may also serve it hot.

Place 2 tablespoons of the roasted fennel seeds, along with the garlic, prunes, and dried apricots in the bowl of a food processor. Process just briefly to combine them. If you are using the Port wine, add it at this point. The mixture will be soft and mushy. To facilitate stuffing the loin, place a piece of plastic wrap on a flat surface and spoon about 1 cup of the prune mixture along the bottom edge. Roll the wrap over the filling to form a long tube shape. Freeze this "tube" until it is solid. Proceed with recipe. Cut the pork loin into pieces 5 or 6 inches long. (Since you will be slicing the meat after it is cooked, it is not necessary to leave the loin whole, and it is much easier to stuff when it is cut into smaller pieces.) Using a sharp knife or a wooden chopstick, poke a hole through the middle of each piece from end to end. Make sure the hole goes all the way through, and be careful not to poke through the sides of the pieces. The hole should be about 1 inch in circumference. Push in the frozen prune filling to fill the hole. You may have to do this from both ends, to make sure you have completely filled the opening. Salt and pepper the filled loin pieces. Heat oven to 375 degrees. Brush a little olive oil on the pieces, and roll each one in the remaining ground roasted fennel seed, making sure to cover the whole surface. Heat the olive oil in a large, heavy sauté pan, and sear the pork loin on all sides to form a crust. Roast for 30-35 minutes at 375 degrees, then at 325 degrees for 20 minutes, or until the internal temperature is 165 degrees. Serve hot or at room temperature with hot turmeric rice (see "Embellishments"), garnished with chopped fresh cilantro.

8 tablespoons dried fennel seed, roasted and ground, divided (see "Basics")

6 cloves garlic, minced

1 cup pitted prunes, chopped

1/2 cup dried apricots, chopped

3 tablespoons Port wine (optional)

2 1/2 to 3 pounds boneless pork loin

1 teaspoon salt and freshly ground pepper to taste

4 tablespoons olive oil

LAMB AND BEAN PILAF

SERVES 6

3 tablespoons olive oil

3 cloves garlic, minced

1 large onion, sliced thinly

1 pound lean lamb, cut into 1 inch cubes (leg or shoulder is fine)

2 cups long grain rice

1 teaspoon each roasted ground cumin, coriander, and allspice (see "Basics")

2 cups chicken or beef stock, plus 1/2 cup in reserve

8 ounces cooked kidney beans

salt and freshly ground pepper to taste

1/4 cup chopped roasted red bell pepper (see "Basics")

2 tablespoons chopped fresh cilantro

What is a "pilaf"? It is a dish of many moods, and simply put, it is rice that is browned in a little oil or butter before it is cooked. It originated in the Near East, and has found its many enhancements throughout the world. In India, the addition of curry plays an important role. In the Middle East, there are infinite combinations of rice with nuts, vegetables, meat, or fish. Sometimes it is called "pilau," and sometimes it is made with bulghur. It is most always cooked with other ingredients, including herbs and spices. Here is a recipe using the excellent lamb from Sparrow Meat Market, along with rice and beans.

In a 3 quart saucepan, heat the oil and sauté the garlic and onions until they are soft. Remove the garlic and onion, and sauté the cubes of lamb over high heat. Return the onions and garlic to the mixture, add the rice, combining well with the meat. Add the cumin, coriander, and allspice, and cook for another minute. Add 2 cups hot stock to the pan. Lower heat, cover, and simmer for 20 minutes. Add the kidney beans, stirring the mixture well. Cover and continue to cook over very low heat for another 10 minutes. If liquid is completely absorbed, add reserved stock, as needed. Taste for seasoning and add salt and freshly ground pepper to taste. Add chopped roasted red pepper and chopped fresh cilantro and serve hot.

TIP: YOU MAY SUBSTITUTE COOKED CHICKPEAS OR COOKED LENTILS FOR THE RED KIDNEY BEANS.

TIP: FOR A SPICIER DISH, ADD HALF OF A MINCED JALAPEÑO PEPPER (OR TO YOUR TASTE) JUST AFTER YOU SAUTÉ THE LAMB CUBES. BE SURE TO REMOVE THE RIBS AND SEEDS FROM THE PEPPER BEFORE YOU MINCE IT.

MERKEL'S BITTER MELON STIR FRY

═══ SERVES 2 ═══

The Ann Arbor Farmers' Market responds to the demands of the community by growing the unusual. For example, George Merkel started growing Asian vegetables some years ago, when it became clear that more and more people were eating and cooking vegetables never before offered there. It is now possible to find a variety of exotic vegetables at the Merkel stand, among others.

Bitter melon is an acquired taste. It has a slightly bitter flavor, as its name indicates, but it is also refreshing. Here is George's recipe for a bitter melon stir fry that can be made with beef or chicken. The melon must be blanched before using in recipes.

To blanche bitter melon, cut the cucumber-size brilliant green vegetable in half lengthwise, seed with a spoon, and scrape away the membrane. It is not necessary to remove the skin. Cut each half diagonally into slices 1/4 inch thick and about 2 inches long. Bring a pot of water to a boil, dump in the cut-up melon, and boil for 2 or 3 minutes. This will remove some of the bitter taste. Drain melon pieces and plunge them into a bowl of cold water to stop the cooking. Drain again and proceed with recipe.

Marinate the steak or chicken with 2 teaspoons soy sauce, ginger, and garlic for 10 to 15 minutes. Heat wok or 12 inch frying pan and, off the burner, spray with Pam, or other spray. Add marinated beef or chicken. Stir fry for a minute and remove from pan. (If you are using chicken, make sure it is not pink.) Spray the pan with Pam again, and add the bitter melon, remaining soy sauce, oyster sauce, and black beans. Add 1 cup of chicken broth and the reserved beef or chicken. Cover, bring to a boil, and simmer 3 minutes. Add enough cornstarch/chicken broth mixture to thicken stir fry to desired consistency. Serve with rice.

TIP: Oyster sauce and salted black beans can be purchased at Asian markets and in some supermarkets.

---

2 medium melons, prepared as described

1/2 pound flank steak, cut into thin strips across the grain OR 2 small chicken breasts, thinly sliced across

3 teaspoons soy sauce, divided

1 teaspoon minced ginger

1 teaspoon minced or pressed garlic

Pam vegetable oil spray or equivalent

1 tablespoon oyster sauce

1 tablespoon salted black beans, rinsed

1 cup chicken broth

2 tablespoons cornstarch mixed with 2 tablespoons chicken broth

MONAHAN'S SPAGHETTI CON LE VONGOLE

8 ounces dry spaghetti or other thin pasta

4 tablespoons olive oil

1 1/2 pounds small littleneck or Manila clams, scrubbed and cleaned

2 large cloves garlic, chopped

4 tablespoons dry white wine

2 tablespoons chopped parsley

salt and freshly ground pepper to taste

Mike Monahan, of the smiling eyes and helpful hints, is the proprietor of the well-known and well-loved fish market at Kerrytown, where you can find just about any edible thing that swims in the ocean, fresh and sparkling. He clearly loves cooking and shares this recipe with us. "Vongole" is Italian for clams, and this classic recipe for pasta and clams is one of his favorites. The succulent Manila clams at Monahan's shop are perfect for this dish.

Cook spaghetti according to directions on package. Heat olive oil in a saucepan over high heat. Add clams and cover. Cook for 2 minutes, shaking pan occasionally. (Most of the clams should be open after 2 minutes.) Then add garlic and parsley and stir. Add the white wine, cover, and cook for another 1 or 2 minutes until all the clams are open. Discard any which do not open. The clams' own juices together with the olive oil and wine make a wonderful sauce. Serve the clams in their shells with sauce over the spaghetti.

Tip: If you are cooking littleneck clams, steam them for 5 minutes or until they open, before proceeding with the recipe.

Tip: To clean clams if they seem gritty, first scrub them under running water. Place clams in a large bowl of cold water in which you have dissolved 1 tablespoon of salt. Let them sit in the water for 2 hours or more in the refrigerator. Drain clams and rinse. They are now ready for cooking.

PASTA WITH SMOKED SALMON AND ARUGULA

SERVES 4

Certain ingredients are sometimes interchangeable and so substitutions don't matter. In this recipe, all the ingredients specified should be used, if possible. Each one does contribute greatly to the whole. "Pasta is pasta," you say. True, but in my estimation, the texture of wide noodles plays nicely against the firm chewiness of thickly sliced smoked salmon. If you can find salmon "bellies," they are even a bit better, being slightly more chewy than the rest of the salmon. Fortunately, both wide noodles, and smoked salmon are easily available at local supermarkets and at Tracklements or Monahan's in the Kerrytown Market.

Bring 4 quarts of water to boil in a large pot. Add the noodles and salt and cook until noodles are soft, about 10 minutes. Drain and toss noodles with olive oil, smoked salmon bits, and arugula. Heat for 5 minutes, or until the arugula is wilted. Add salt and freshly ground black pepper to taste. Divide among 4 heated bowls or plates and serve hot.

Tip: Salmon "bellies," which are the bottom of the fillet, are quite fatty and chewy and because of this their flavor does not get lost when served with the noodles.

Tip: For another taste dimension, serve a bowl of 4% cottage cheese along with this, and each diner can pile on his own. The combination of cold cottage cheese and hot noodles is terrific.

1 pound extra wide noodles (about 1/2 inch wide)

1 teaspoon salt

1 tablespoon olive oil

8 ounces thickly sliced smoked salmon cut into 2 inch pieces or salmon"bellies," cut into 1/4 inch wide bits

1 pound arugula, washed, tough stems removed

salt and freshly ground black pepper to taste

PAUL SAGINAW'S ROOT RISOTTO

5 tablespoons butter, divided

1 tablespoon olive oil

1/2 cup diced rutabaga

1/2 cup diced celery root

1/2 cup diced parsnip

1/4 red bell pepper, diced

1/4 orange bell pepper, diced

1/4 yellow bell pepper, diced

5 cups vegetable broth
(see "Soups")

2 cloves garlic, minced

1/2 small onion, diced

1 1/2 cups Arborio rice

1 teaspoon salt

3 ounces mozzarella cheese,
grated

Watching Paul Saginaw's face as he describes this dish helps us understand why Zingerman's is such a great store. The passion for flavor and perfection is in his face as he speaks. The butter must be the best, the Italian rice the most perfect, and the colors must balance and blend seamlessly with the fresh mozzarella cheese. How could it not be superb? Paul serves this with the skinny string beans the French call "haricots verts," which are available both at the Farmers' Market and at the indoor market, Zingerman's Practical Produce, at Kerrytown.

Melter butter in a medium size sauté pan. Add olive oil and sauté the rutabaga, celery root, parsnips, and red and yellow peppers until they are tender, and not mushy. Remove from the pan and set aside. Heat vegetable broth and keep warm. Melt remaining butter in a 2 quart saucepan. Sauté the garlic and onion in the butter until soft. Add rice, and stir to coat all the grains with the butter. Add the salt. Add the vegetable stock, 1/2 cup at a time. Stir once or twice. Do not cover the pot. As the stock is absorbed by the rice, add more. Continue in this manner until the rice is slightly soft, and there is still about 1 cup of stock left. Add the remaining stock and cook just until the rice is "al dente", each grain retaining a slightly hard whitish center, while the outside is soft. Taste for seasonings, adding additional salt and freshly ground pepper as needed. Spoon mixture into a warmed serving bowl and mix in the diced rutabaga, celery root, parsnips and peppers along with the grated mozzarella cheese.

RALPH SNOW'S
MAPLE BARBECUED SPARERIBS

Who (except our vegetarian friends) doesn't like spareribs? Those sloppy, toothsome, appetizing ribs drip all over the front of your shirt onto the tablecloth, and you wonder how you ate them so quickly, and did you have your share? My advice? Eat them only with relatives or close friends, wear old clothes, and have plenty of napkins at hand. The addition of maple syrup to the cooking is an inspired innovation.

Place spareribs in a large pot with enough water to cover. Bring to a boil, reduce heat and simmer for 30 minutes. Drain. Mix the remaining ingredients together in a small bowl. Heat oven to 350 degrees. Place spareribs in a shallow pan and pour about half of the maple sauce over the ribs. Bake 30 minutes, or until tender. Turn and baste occasionally with the remaining sauce for another 10 minutes. Broil 5 minutes to finish browning. A bowl of coleslaw and some good bread to soak up the drippings, and where are you? Heaven!

3 pounds spareribs

3/4 cup maple syrup

1 tablespoon ketchup

1 tablespoon cider vinegar

1 teaspoon finely chopped onion

1 teaspoon Worcestershire sauce

1 teaspoon salt

1/4 teaspoon mustard powder

1/8 teaspoon black pepper

ROAST LEG OF LAMB

SERVES 8-10

6 pound leg of lamb

6-8 cloves of peeled garlic, slivered

8-10 anchovy fillets

2 tablespoons olive oil

**3 tablespoons za'atar (available in middle eastern markets)
OR
2 tablespoons dried thyme mixed with 1 tablespoon roasted cumin (see "Basics")**

24-30 shelled pistachio nuts

salt and freshly ground pepper to taste

Some years ago, when I knew I was going to be in New York city, I would arrange to have a private lesson with James Beard. I always learned something, and I always enjoyed myself. In those days I used to think that if the recipe wasn't French, it wasn't special. I didn't realize then that I was privileged to be learning from one of the great American culinary heroes. Having grown older, wiser, more sure of myself and proud of American cooking, I offer this recipe, which I learned from him, with a few additions of my own. Za'atar is a middle eastern mixture of herbs. Although it is not quite the same, you may substitute a mixture of dried thyme and roasted cumin for the za'atar. It's easy to make. Don't be put off by the addition of anchovies. They completely dissolve in the cooking and impart a saltiness to the lamb that seems just right. Sparrow's Meat Market in Kerrytown, or your favorite butcher can bone the lamb leg, if you like. I personally like to cook it on the bone, as it develops a richer flavor while roasting.

Heat oven to 350 degrees. Make deep slits all over the leg of lamb and insert slivers of garlic, anchovy fillets, and pistachio nuts.

Rub the meat with the olive oil, za'atar or mixture of dried thyme and cumin, salt and freshly ground black pepper. Place on a rack in a roasting pan and roast for 1 hour. Check the internal temperature and when it registers 125 to 130 degrees, it is done. This may take another 30 minutes, so test every 10 minutes, remembering that the meat will continue to cook after you remove it from the oven. This cooking should result in a pink inside. Allow the meat to stand for 10 or 15 minutes before you carve it.

SAUTÉED GARLIC SHRIMP WITH FRESH CILANTRO

SERVES 4

Shrimp and garlic seem to have an affinity for each other. Usually, it is parsley, bread crumbs, and garlic which form the mortar to build many shrimp dishes. Here I have featured cilantro, which is quite pungent, instead of parsley, and although it may be an acquired taste for some, I think it works very well when balanced with Balsamic vinegar or lemon juice.

Heat olive oil in a large sauté pan. Add shrimp and cook until opaque, about 1 minute. Add minced garlic and cook another 15 seconds. Add salt, pepper, and bread crumbs. Cook another 30 seconds. Add vinegar or lemon juice, then turn off heat. Toss in the chopped cilantro, mixing well. Serve while hot with cooked angel hair pasta tossed with a little olive oil, or Turmeric Rice (see "Embellishments").

TIP: IF YOU NEED A LITTLE MORE OLIVE OIL TO KEEP THE BREAD CRUMBS FROM BURNING, ADD 1 OR 2 TABLESPOONS JUST BEFORE YOU ADD THE CRUMBS.

2 tablespoons extra virgin olive oil

1 pound (21-25) shrimp, peeled and deveined

3 cloves garlic, minced or pressed

1/2 cup fresh bread crumbs

1/2 teaspoon salt and freshly ground pepper to taste

2 tablespoons Balsamic vinegar or 1 tablespoon lemon juice

1/2 cup chopped fresh cilantro

SOUTHWEST CORN PONE

SERVES 10

1 tablespoon canola, olive, or corn oil

1 jalapeño pepper, seeded and diced

1 red bell pepper, chopped

1 large Spanish onion, chopped

2 cloves garlic, minced

1 teaspoon chili powder (or more, to taste)

salt and freshly ground pepper to taste

4 cups cooked beans of your choice (not too dry—black, kidney, pinto, etc.)

1 small package frozen corn

2 cups cornmeal

2 teaspoons baking soda

1 teaspoon salt

4 tablespoons melted margarine or butter

1 quart buttermilk

2 eggs, slightly beaten

Some of us remember 25 years ago when the People's Food Co-op was just starting. It was a small, rather scruffy looking, albeit clean place, staffed by an earnest looking group, eager to provide pesticide-free food that had received a minimum of processing and refining and that was locally produced. It is still following these precepts, now in a brightly lit and mirrored shop. Corn pone, a southern dish, is usually an eggless cornbread that is shaped into small ovals and fried, so some liberty is taken with the name, but here is a recipe which, as its creator, People's Food Co-op's Kevin Sharp says," is a southwest version of a down-home favorite-and is great on winter days."

Heat oven to 450 degrees. Lightly grease a 9 inch x 13 inch baking dish. Using a medium sized sauté pan, heat oil and add diced jalapeño and red bell peppers, chopped onion, and garlic. Cook for five minutes, or until soft, turning the mixture frequently to avoid scorching. Add the chili power, salt, freshly ground pepper, cooked beans, and corn. Continue to cook until heated through. Pour into greased baking dish.

In a large bowl, combine the corn meal, baking soda, baking powder, and salt. In another bowl, combine the melted margarine or butter, buttermilk, and beaten eggs. Stir the wet and dry ingredients together just until they are incorporated. Pour this batter over the bean/corn mixture and bake on the top rack of oven until topping is golden brown, approximately 30 minutes.

SPINACH PIE

SERVES 8-10

It's not by accident that many cultures have at least one dough-related spinach recipe. Sometimes the spinach is encased in filo dough, sometimes it fits snugly into a pie dough turnover. Sometimes it is embellished with bits of meat or hard-boiled eggs. Where spinach is, its dough companion is not far behind. The addition of herbs to the dough adds a little zing to the pie, and although this recipe calls for fresh spinach, you can substitute three (10 ounce) packages of frozen, chopped spinach, thawed and completely drained of water.

Place flour, butter, dill, and salt in the bowl of a food processor. Process briefly until the mixture becomes coarse and crumbly. Add water little by little and process some more, just until the dough comes together. Remove it from the processor and dust with flour. Divide dough into two parts and wrap it in plastic wrap or place it in a plastic bag. Chill in refrigerator for 30 minutes to allow the gluten to expand and become elastic. If you choose to make this dough well ahead, then let it soften a bit at room temperature before you attempt to roll it out.

Wash spinach in several changes of cold water and remove heavy stems. Place the leaves in a large pot with 1/2 cup cold water. Cover pot and cook for approximately 5 minutes, or until the spinach is wilted. To set the color of the spinach, remove it from the pot and plunge it into a large bowl of very cold water. Drain thoroughly, squeezing out remaining water. Chop spinach coarsely. Heat olive oil in a large sauté pan and cook onions until they are soft. Combine onions with chopped spinach and add salt, pepper, and nutmeg.

Heat oven to 350 degrees. Brush an 8 or 9 inch springform pan with olive oil. Roll out half of the dough into a circle of about 14 inches diameter. Roll out the remaining dough to a 9 inch circle. Fix the larger circle of dough into the pan and add the spinach mixture. With a soup spoon, make 6 depressions in the filling. Break the eggs one at a time and fill each depression with one egg. Cover the filling with the remaining circle of dough and crimp the edges of the two layers of dough together. Beat the egg yolk with the cream or milk and brush the mixture over the top of the dough. Cut a cross into the dough, and roll back the edges to vent the pie. Bake about 1 hour or until top of dough is golden. This can be eaten hot or at room temperature.

TIP: FOR A DIFFERENT FLAVOR, ADD 1 CUP OF THINLY SLICED FENNEL BULB, SAUTÉED ALONG WITH THE ONION, AND SUBSTITUTE 1 TABLESPOON GROUND ROASTED FENNEL SEED (SEE "BASICS") FOR THE FRESH DILL IN THE CRUST.

4 cups all purpose flour

1 1/2 cups unsalted butter

2 tablespoons chopped fresh dill

1/2 teaspoon salt

3 or 4 tablespoons cold water

3 pounds fresh spinach, cleaned and drained

2 tablespoons extra virgin olive oil

3 cups chopped sweet onions

2 cloves garlic, minced or pressed

1/2 teaspoon salt and freshly ground black pepper

1/4 teaspoon ground nutmeg

6 whole eggs

1 egg yolk mixed with 2 tablespoons cream or milk

CAROL'S SQUASH ENCHILADAS

SERVES 3-4

1 medium-sized delicata, sweet dumpling, or other winter squash

1 tablespoon olive oil

1/2 cup chopped scallions or onions

2-3 cloves garlic, minced

4 ounces soft goat cheese

1/2 each red and yellow bell peppers, diced and sautéed

1/2 teaspoon ground cumin

salt and freshly ground pepper to taste

vegetable spray

6 whole wheat tortillas (or lawash)

2 1/2 to 3 cups salsa (see "Side Dishes")

Carol Collins, manager of People's Food Co-op, says that goat cheese makes these enchiladas very special, but you may substitute cream cheese, according to Sharon Barbour, outreach and education manager. Include red or yellow bell peppers as part of the sautéed vegetables, and you will have a tantalizing entrée. Lawash (sometimes called "lavosh") is a Middle Eastern thin bread which is pliable enough to roll, like tortillas.

Heat oven to 350 degrees. Cut squash in half, scooping out the seeds. Place it in a pan cut side down, then bake for 30-45 minutes, or until soft. Heat oil in a medium size sauté pan and cook the scallions or onions and minced garlic until soft. Set aside. Scoop the pulp of the cooked squash into a bowl and add the goat cheese while squash is still warm. Add the sautéed scallions or onions, garlic, peppers, ground cumin, and salt and pepper. Spray a shallow casserole dish or pan with vegetable oil spray. Spoon filling onto tortillas or lawash and roll them up. Place seam side down into pan and cover with plenty of tomato salsa (see "Side Dishes"). Cover and bake for 30 minutes. Serve on a bed of brown rice.

SQUASH, SAGE, AND GINGER RICE WITH ITALIAN SAUSAGE

SERVES 6 AS A MAIN COURSE

Acorn, Hubbard, or any similar winter squash combines with fresh sage and ginger to create a dish that is both savory and aromatic. Winter squash is always available, and you may use any type of sausage, although a spicy, highly seasoned one seems to balance very well with the other ingredients.

Heat olive oil and butter in a 3 quart saucepan. Add the crumbled Italian sausage. Sauté for another 5 minutes, stirring frequently. Add minced onion and garlic, and sauté until soft. Mix in the dried sage. Add the squash and the minced and dried ginger. Cook for a few minutes. Add the rice, and stir to coat all of the grains with oil. Add the hot chicken stock, reduce heat, and cook, covered, about 20 minutes. Turn off heat, and steam for another ten minutes, covered. Add 3/4 cup of the grated Parmesan Reggiano cheese and the fresh sage and mix well. Spoon the rice into warm bowls. Pass the remaining grated cheese.

TIP: THE USE OF BOTH DRIED AND FRESH SAGE WILL GIVE A NICE BOOST OF FLAVOR TO THE RICE. TASTE FOR SEASONING. YOU MAY WANT TO ADD SOME SALT AND PEPPER, OR MORE CHOPPED FRESH SAGE.

TIP: IF YOU FEEL EXTRAVAGANT, PURCHASE SOME WHITE TRUFFLE OIL AT ZINGERMAN'S. A FEW DROPS ADDED JUST BEFORE SERVING MAKES THIS TASTE TRULY HEAVENLY.

TIP: FOR A VEGETARIAN ENTRÉE OMIT THE SAUSAGE ENTIRELY. STRIPS OF COOKED OMELET COULD PROVIDE A BIT OF PROTEIN, IF DESIRED.

2 tablespoons olive oil

3 tablespoons butter

1/2 pound Italian sausage, removed from casing, crumbled

3/4 cup minced onion

3 or 4 cloves garlic, minced

1 tablespoon dried sage

1 1/2 cups peeled and diced acorn squash

2 tablespoons minced or grated fresh ginger

1 teaspoon dried ginger

2 cups long grain rice

3 1/2 cups hot chicken or vegetable stock

1/2 teaspoon salt

1 cup grated Parmesan Reggiano cheese

3 tablespoons fresh sage, chopped

SWISS CHARD SOUFFLÉ

SERVES 6

3 tablespoons olive oil

2 tablespoons dry bread crumbs mixed with 3 tablespoons grated Parmesan cheese

1/2 cup minced onion

2 cloves garlic, minced

1 pound Swiss chard, chopped

1/4 teaspoon cayenne pepper (optional)

2 cups ricotta, part skim

3 tablespoons flour

salt and freshly ground pepper to taste

1 tablespoon dried thyme

4 egg whites, preferably room temperature

Don't be intimidated by soufflés. They are easy to prepare and wonderful to behold. Versatility is the soufflé's middle name. It can be an appetizer, side dish, main course, or dessert. It usually can be put together in less than 30 minutes, and is often a perfect, low fat, luxurious way to use up leftovers. Here we use Swiss chard, but you can also use spinach, or any other leafy green of your choice.

Use some of the olive oil to grease an 8 cup soufflé mold and dust it with the mixture of bread crumbs and grated Parmesan cheese. Heat oven to 425 degrees. Heat remaining oil in a large sauté pan and cook the garlic and onions until they are soft but not brown. Wash well, then drain the chopped Swiss chard and add it to the sauté pan. Continue to cook until it is quite wilted. This should take about 5-8 minutes. Process the cooked mixture in a food processor until it is almost a purée. Add the cayenne pepper, ricotta, flour, salt, freshly ground pepper, and dried thyme. In a separate bowl, beat the egg whites until they hold a soft peak. Stir about 1/3 of the beaten egg whites into the Swiss chard mixture. Add this to the remaining egg whites by folding the mixture gently. Pour into the prepared soufflé mold and bake for 20 minutes. At this point, turn heat down to 375 degrees and continue to bake another 20-25 minutes, or until the soufflé is light brown and puffy. Serve with Fresh Tomato Sauce (see "Sauces").

TIP: THE SOUFFLÉ MAY BE PREPARED A DAY OR TWO AHEAD UP TO THE POINT OF BEATING THE EGG WHITES. WHEN READY TO COOK, ALL YOU HAVE TO DO IS HEAT UP THE OVEN, BEAT THE EGG WHITES, AND COMBINE THEM WITH THE SOLIDS.

TRACKLEMENTS
SMOKED SALMON CAKES

=== SERVES 4 ===

This is not your mother's salmon cake. This recipe presents a new twist on the old-fashioned salmon croquette. T. R. Durham of Tracklements in Kerrytown opens new vistas to the palate with his innovative addition of herb and spice mixtures to his elegant smoked salmon. He has provided us with this recipe which features his terrific smoked salmon. Serve it with Roasted Red Pepper Sauce (see "Sauces"), and Spinach Ambrosia (see "Side Dishes").

Slice the salmon away from the skin, and chop into small pieces. Use a fork to mix the salmon with the remaining ingredients, except the oil and lemon wedges. With your hands, carefully shape the mixture into eight cakes. Heat oil in a sauté pan large enough to hold all the salmon cakes without touching. When oil is hot, sauté the fish cakes about three minutes on each side, or until they are golden brown and heated through. Garnish with lemon wedges and serve with the Roasted Red Pepper Sauce (see "Sauces").

TIP: FOR ADDED FLAVOR, ADD 1/4 CUP CAPERS AND CHOPPED HOT JALAPEÑO OR CHERRY PEPPERS TO THE SALMON MIXTURE AND 1 TABLESPOON PURCHASED MAYONNAISE TO THE SAUCE.

1/2 to 3/4 pound smoked salmon (cheaper end cut, if available)

1/2 cup dry white bread crumbs

1 egg, lightly beaten

1 medium onion, finely chopped

1 large clove garlic, finely chopped

4 tablespoons chopped parsley

juice of 1 lemon

dash of hot sauce, to taste

freshly ground black pepper

1 tablespoon vegetable oil

1 lemon, cut into wedges, for garnish

TWO WAY SCALLOPS

SERVES 6

1 1/2 pounds small bay or large sea scallops

3 tablespoons extra virgin olive oil

2 tablespoons lime juice

2 tablespoons white wine vinegar

2 teaspoons seeded and minced fresh jalapeño pepper

3 cloves garlic, minced or pressed

2 teaspoons chopped fresh oregano

2 tablespoons thinly sliced scallion rings, white and green parts

3 teaspoons finely diced purple onion

2 tablespoons chopped cilantro

cilantro sprigs and thin lime slices (optional)

What a versatile recipe this is! The marinade serves as both a cooking medium and a flavoring agent. If you want to present the scallops as a cold appetizer called "seviche," use the small bay scallops and eliminate the cooking. The marinade will "cook" or "cure" the raw scallops. (As with any fish, be sure to use high quality for freshness and safety.) If you grill, broil, or pan sear the scallops, use the largest you can find. In testing this recipe, I used really large ones— approximately 16 scallops to the pound.

If you are using the large scallops and plan to broil or grill them, soak enough wooden skewers in cold water to allow for 3 or 4 scallops per skewer.

Rinse scallops and pat dry. Using a large bowl, combine the scallops with the remaining ingredients (except the optional cilantro and lime slices), and chill them for at least four hours. If you are using the small scallops as a seviche, they are now ready to be eaten. Serve them on individual plates on a bed of greens, or in a serving bowl as part of a buffet. If you are using sea scallops, they are now ready for cooking. Discard the marinade and thread the scallops on the pre-soaked skewers. Grill them for 2 minutes on a side, or pan sear them in a little olive oil over medium high heat. Garnish with cilantro sprigs and lime slices and serve with Turmeric Rice (see "Embellishments").

TIP: IF YOU SCORE THE LARGE SCALLOPS WITH ABOUT A 1/4 INCH CROSSHATCH ON ONE SIDE, THEY WILL NOT ONLY LOOK PRETTY, BUT WILL COOK FASTER.

SIDE DISHES

The wonderful thing about side dishes is that they can also masquerade as lunch, brunch, or appetizer. Here are seventeen recipes that can do just that. Spinach pie, hearty enough to stand on its own, cauliflower gratin, gorgeous and delectable, asparagus with ginger sauce, potato cheese puff, and braised lettuce with oyster sauce will brighten any menu. Make a meal of scalloped tomatoes and peas with prosciutto, or nibble on some roasted herbed vegetables, and you will appreciate once more what treasures we have in the Ann Arbor Farmers' Market and Kerrytown market area.

ASPARAGUS WITH GINGER SAUCE

═══ SERVES 4-6 ═══

1 1/2 pounds asparagus, tough ends removed, peeled up to base of tips

1/2 cup milk

1/2 cup chicken stock

2 teaspoons cornstarch

1 teaspoon grated fresh ginger

1 tablespoon chopped fresh lemon grass, white part only

1/2 teaspoon shredded lemon zest

This is a heady dish, with its sauce of ginger and fresh lemon grass acting as a fine counterpoint to the buttery asparagus. Whether you like your asparagus pencil thin, or pleasingly plump, the market is there for you. Serve asparagus with lightly breaded and sautéed fish fillets and scalloped tomatoes. The plentiful Farmers' Market asparagus makes this dish a superb treat in early spring, but even winter asparagus are refreshed by the perfume of the sauce.

Line up the asparagus so the tips are even. Cut off the woody ends so the stalks are an even length. Using a vegetable peeler, peel each stalk of asparagus from the base of the tip to the bottom. Immerse asparagus in water as each stalk is peeled. Using a large sauté pan or flat flame-proof casserole, bring 2 quarts of water to the boil with 1/2 teaspoon salt. Add the asparagus, laying them flat in the pan. Cover the pan and reduce heat. Remove them as soon as they are tender, about 5 minutes, and immerse them immediately in cold water to set the color. Drain and set aside.

Using a 1 quart sauce pan, heat the milk and all but 2 tablespoons chicken stock. Dissolve the cornstarch in the remaining 2 tablespoons chicken stock and add it to the heated milk. Stir as it thickens. Add the fresh ginger, lemon grass, and lemon zest, and stir to mix.

Reheat asparagus, covered, either in microwave for 2 minutes, or by immersing them in boiling water for 2 minutes. (Be sure to drain them.) Place in a warmed serving dish and pour the sauce over them. Serve as a first course, or as a side dish with poached salmon.

Tip: If you have any sauce left, it is very good mixed with hot pasta—and low fat, too.

Tip: Lemon grass, a member of the citronella family, is found in many Asian markets, usually stored in a large bucket of water, root end down.

BRAISED LETTUCE WITH OYSTER SAUCE

=== SERVES 6-8 ===

This is a somewhat unusual recipe, but one that always delights and surprises. We rarely think of cooking lettuce, but somehow this seems like just the right thing to eat with plain poached or steamed chicken breast or salmon. It dresses up a meal and is not too difficult to make. Oyster sauce is available bottled in some supermarkets and most Asian food stores. It adds a really nice touch to the blandness of the lettuce.

Heat oven to 350 degrees. Trim bottom edge of each head of lettuce, but leave it whole. Heat about 1 gallon of water in a large pot. Fill a large bowl with very cold water and ice (or use a clean sink), and when water has reached a rolling boil, plunge 2 or 3 heads of lettuce at a time into the pot. Cook for 30 seconds, then remove with tongs and place them immediately into the cold water. Proceed with the rest of the lettuce. Drain heads thoroughly, then fold each one in two the long way. Squeeze each one into a roundish shape with your hands. Make sure they are drained completely. Set aside.

Heat olive oil in an oven-proof casserole. Add the diced bacon if you are using it and sauté until tender, not crisp. Sauté the onions, carrots, and garlic to a wilted state. Remove the cooked vegetables from the casserole and arrange the heads of lettuce in one layer in the casserole. Strew the cooked vegetables and bacon over the top of the lettuce. Cover with a piece of waxed paper and then aluminum foil. Heat in oven for 20 to 30 minutes. About 5 minutes before serving, combine the olive oil and oyster sauce in a small saucepan and bring to a simmer. Pour sauce over lettuce balls just before serving.

TIP: YOU CAN SUBSTITUTE REAL BACON "BITS" (AVAILABLE IN JARS) FOR THE COOKED BACON. STIR ABOUT 3 TABLESPOONS, RIGHT FROM THE JAR, INTO THE COOKED VEGETABLES JUST BEFORE YOU PLACE THEM INTO THE OVEN.

6-8 heads of romaine or escarolle lettuce, rinsed and drained

1 teaspoon salt

2 tablespoons olive oil

2 thick (1/4 inch) slices slab bacon, cut into small dice (optional)

1 large onion, sliced

1 carrot, cleaned and sliced into 1/4 inch rounds

2 cloves garlic, minced

1/2 teaspoon salt and freshly ground pepper to taste

4 tablespoons olive oil

2 tablespoons oyster sauce

DUKE AND LINDA DONAHEE'S
ZUCCHINI CAKES

YIELD: ABOUT 8 PATTIES

2 cups grated zucchini

4 eggs, beaten

1 cup corn meal

1/2 cup chopped onion

1/2 teaspoon salt and freshly ground pepper to taste

2 tablespoons vegetable oil

2 tomatoes, sliced into 1/4 inch rounds

8 thin slices Cheddar cheese

Call them cakes, patties, or pancakes, here is another zucchini recipe that brightens a meal. Sautéing them first gives them a crispy crust, and finishing them in the oven with a crown of tomato and cheese extends the dish and turns it into a hearty vegetarian entree.

Heat oven to 350 degrees. Combine grated zucchini, beaten eggs, corn meal, and chopped onion. Add salt and pepper to taste. Heat oil in a large sauté pan, or on a hot griddle. Spoon mixture, about 1/2 cup at a time, onto the pan. Fry until golden brown. Turn patties once, to brown the other side. Place the browned patties on a cookie sheet and top with a slice of tomato and a slice of cheese. Place in preheated oven until cheese is melted.

TIP: FOR A DIFFERENT SLANT, ADD 1 TABLESPOON GROUND ROASTED CUMIN SEEDS TO THE MIXTURE BEFORE SAUTÉING (SEE "BASICS").

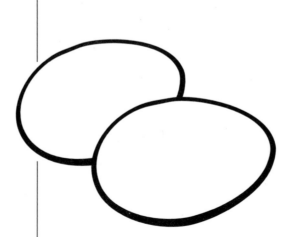

FRESH TOMATO SALSA

SERVES 4

Salsa is the Spanish word for sauce, cooked or fresh. On the American culinary scene, salsa is taken to mean the cold version, most often made with a mixture of fresh vegetables punctuated by a spicy sauce and eaten with Mexican food. This is the version presented here, although there are many variations. Several growers at the Farmers' Market sell tomatillos, and many sell plum tomatoes, fresh cilantro, jalapeño peppers, and onions. Even though this is technically a sauce, I like to use it as an accompaniment to fish or poached chicken, or as a blanket for Squash Enchiladas (see "Entrees").

Combine all ingredients and marinate in refrigerator overnight, or at least 3 hours. Taste and correct seasoning to your liking.

TIP: ADD OTHER VEGETABLES OR FRUITS FOR VARIATION: COOKED BLACK BEANS, CORN, AND DICED FRESH PEACHES AND PLUMS ARE EXCELLENT CHOICES.

TIP: TOMATILLOS, WHICH BELONG TO THE NIGHTSHADE FAMILY, LOOK LIKE SMALL GREEN TOMATOES WITH A THIN, PAPERLIKE HUSK. THEY ARE RELATED TO THE CAPE GOOSEBERRY AND ARE PALE YELLOW WHEN RIPE, ALTHOUGH THEY ARE USUALLY EATEN WHEN THEY ARE GREEN.

---

6 plum tomatoes, blanched, seeded, diced (see "Basics")

12 medium-size tomatillos, husks removed, cut into large dice

3 cloves garlic, minced or pressed

1 jalapeño pepper, seeds removed, minced

4 tablespoons chopped sweet onion

4 tablespoons chopped fresh cilantro

1 teaspoon hot sauce (or to taste)

1/2 teaspoon salt and freshly ground pepper to taste

2 tablespoons olive oil (optional)

3 tablespoons white vinegar

FRIED GREEN TOMATOES

SERVES 6

3 or 4 green tomatoes

1 cup cornmeal

1/2 cup grated Parmesan Reggiano cheese (optional)

1 teaspoon salt and freshly ground pepper to taste

5 tablespoons vegetable oil or olive oil

Along with the end of harvest time, comes a big question: After pickles and chutney, where can we go with green tomatoes? It's not a world-shaking question, and here is an obvious answer. Fried green tomatoes are simple to prepare, and vanish as soon as you serve them, so be sure to make plenty.

Slice tomatoes into 1/2 inch slices. Mix cornmeal, Parmesan cheese, salt and pepper together. Heat vegetable oil or olive oil in a 12 inch sauté pan. Dip tomato slices into the cornmeal mixture, making sure they are well covered. Sauté the slices in the heated oil, on both sides, about 2 minutes on each side. Drain on paper toweling.

TIP: THE ADDITION OF GRATED CHEESE TO THE COATING MIX IS UNCONVENTIONAL, BUT DELICIOUS. THIS DISH GOES VERY WELL WITH ANY STEAMED OR POACHED FISH, OR IF YOU'VE REALLY LOST ALL CONTROL, SOUTHERN FRIED CHICKEN, OR DEEP-FRIED ANYTHING. MAKE SURE TO USE LOTS OF BLACK PEPPER.

CAULIFLOWER GRATIN WITH CURRY

I frequently make variations of this recipe for my own table. It is so simple to make and so satisfying that I often fall back on making it when I want something substantial that's not a potato. The end of summer brings us huge cauliflower, and their size does not affect their tenderness or their taste. When puréed, as in this recipe, cauliflower takes on a whole new identity.

Break cauliflower into golf ball-size pieces, removing any leaves and tough stems. Cover pieces with water in a large pot and add salt. Bring water to a boil, then turn heat down to maintain a simmer. Partially cover the pot, and cook until cauliflower is soft, but not mushy. Heat oven to 350 degrees. Drain cauliflower pieces and put them back in pot to cook for 1 minute. (This will dry up any water still clinging to the cauliflower.) Using a food processor, purée the cauliflower, along with the milk or cream, until it is smooth. Do not purée all of the pieces in one batch, as some of it will turn gummy before it is all done. Purée a little at a time, and then remove it to a bowl as you proceed. Mix in the curry powder while the purée is still warm. Add salt and freshly ground black pepper to taste. Spray a flat gratin dish (large enough to contain the purée to at least a 1 inch depth) with vegetable oil and pour in the cauliflower mixture. Sprinkle grated cheese over the top and bake for 30 minutes, or until the top is crusty and brown.

TIP: FOR A FLAVOR CHANGE, OMIT THE CURRY AND THE PARMESAN CHEESE, ADD 2 TEASPOONS OF WHITE TRUFFLE OIL TO THE PURÉE, AND DOT TOP WITH 1 TABLESPOON BUTTER.

TIP: IF YOU LIKE A LOT OF CRUST, USE A WIDE GRATIN DISH, BUT BE SURE TO FILL IT TO A DEPTH HIGH ENOUGH SO THE PURÉE WON'T DRY OUT BEFORE IT IS HEATED THROUGH——1 INCH, AT LEAST.

---

1 medium size cauliflower

1/2 teaspoon salt

1/2 cup 2% milk or half and half

1 teaspoon curry powder, or to taste

salt and freshly ground black pepper to taste

vegetable oil spray

1 cup grated Parmesan Reggiano cheese (optional)

JULIENNE OF VEGETABLES

═══ SERVES 6 ═══

3 large zucchini, whole

6 large carrots, blanched, whole

2 red peppers, roasted and peeled

2 tablespoons extra virgin olive oil

2 large leeks, white part only, julienned

2 cloves garlic, minced or pressed

**1 cup chopped aromatics, such as a mixture of fresh parsley, chives and cilantro
OR
a mixture of dried oregano, rosemary and thyme to equal 1 tablespoon**

So, what is a julienne? Simply stated, to julienne any food is to cut it into matchstick shapes. Here is a colorful melange of vegetables that can accompany almost any entrée. They can be placed on the plate as a base of presentation, arranged around the main entrée, or served on the side. Use your imagination—these herbs and selection of vegetables are just suggestions. Summertime brings a myriad of choices. Be an artist, have fun.

Cut zucchini and carrots into lengthwise slices, 1/4 inch thick and approximately 3 inches long, using a mandoline, or similar vegetable slicer. Or to julienne by hand; stack thin (1/4 inch thick) slices of zucchini, and cut each stack into as many thin strips as the width of the slices will allow. Do the same with the blanched carrots slices. The red peppers must be sliced by hand, as they are too soft to be run through the mandoline. Heat olive oil in a large deep sauté pan and add leeks and garlic. If using dried aromatics, add them at this stage. When leeks are soft, add the julienned carrots. Cook until slightly crunchy. Add zucchini and cook another 2 or 3 minutes. Add red peppers, and toss all the vegetables together until they are evenly distributed. If fresh aromatics are being used, add them at this point. Taste for seasonings, and add salt and pepper, if necessary.

TIP: Any combination of vegetables may be used: Celeriac, shiitake mushrooms, yellow pepper strips, green beans, etc. Make sure to cut them into approximately the same size strips.

TIP: This dish can be prepared entirely in advance, and reheated in a microwave oven, covered, for 2 minutes on high.

MISSISSIPPI CORN AND OKRA

SERVES 4-6

Here's a snappy idea. I've heard it said that one has to grow up with okra in order to like, or even tolerate, it. Don't be hesitant, try it. Remember to pare the top of it, without breaking the skin. This avoids some of the viscosity which you may find unpalatable. Also, be sure to purchase okra whose striations are not dark. They may have been sitting around for a while, and are not very fresh. Corn and okra laced with a red pepper sauce makes for a lively dish. Add this to baked lemon chicken breasts or Sautéed Garlic Shrimp (see "Entrees"), and you'll have a colorful, tasty meal.

Heat olive oil in a medium-sized saucepan. Add the chopped onion and garlic and cook together for 1 minute. Blanche okra while the pods are whole, but the caps are trimmed. Cut into slices after blanching. (To blanche the okra, bring 1 quart of salted water to a boil and toss in the okra. Cook for 1 minute. Using a slotted spoon, or strainer, remove the okra from the boiling water and plunge it into a large bowl of iced water to stop the cooking. Drain, and continue with recipe.) Add corn, okra and chicken stock or water to the sauté pan. Cover and turn heat to low. Cook for 5 minutes, or until okra is tender-crisp. Drain liquids, and add salt, pepper, hot sauce, and 1 teaspoon butter.

1 tablespoon olive oil

2 tablespoons chopped onion

1 tablespoon minced or pressed garlic

2 cups trimmed okra, blanched, cut into 1/4"rounds

2 cups fresh cooked corn, cut from the cob

1/3 cup chicken stock or water

1/2 teaspoon salt and freshly ground pepper to taste

Tabasco, or equivalent hot sauce to taste

1 teaspoon butter

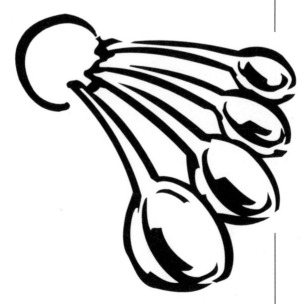

OKRA, PROSCIUTTO, SUN-DRIED TOMATOES, AND SHALLOTS

SERVES 4

2 tablespoons olive oil

2 cloves garlic, minced or pressed

1/2 medium onion, diced

2 shallots, diced

2 cups small pods okra, washed and trimmed

3 or 4 sun dried tomatoes

1 teaspoon dried oregano

2 tablespoon fresh oregano, chopped

1/2 teaspoon salt and freshly ground black pepper to taste

3 ounces thinly sliced prosciutto, chopped

2 tablespoons Balsamic vinegar

Okra marries well with strips of prosciutto, sun-dried tomatoes, and shallots, producing a savory side dish or topping for pasta. Choose the smallest okra you can find, as they are the most tender. This dish goes well with roast lamb; when it is coarsely chopped, it provides a tasty and unusual filling for an omelet. If you cannot find prosciutto, a seasoned, salt-cured, air-dried, ham imported from Italy, use the domestic variety which is available in some supermarkets, or substitute cooked, crumbled bacon. I add the prosciutto just before serving, to retain its delicate texture.

Heat olive oil in a 12 inch sauté pan. Add garlic, diced onion, and shallots. Cook for a few minutes to blend the flavors. Add the okra, sun-dried tomatoes, the dried and fresh oregano, salt and pepper. Cook over medium heat for 10-15 minutes, or until the okra is just slightly crunchy. Add the chopped prosciutto and vinegar, and cook another 30 seconds. This small amount of vinegar helps blend the flavors of the dried herbs and fresh vegetables, imparting a luscious quality to the finished recipe.

TIP: THE FLAVOR OF SHALLOTS IS A BIT MORE SUBTLE THAN ONION, AND NOT AS HARSH AS GARLIC. SO WHY USE SHALLOTS HERE, WHEN ONIONS AND GARLIC ARE ALSO PRESENT? BECAUSE THE INTERPLAY IS LIKE THREE STRINGS ON A MUSICAL INSTRUMENT, EACH PROVIDING ITS OWN NOTE BUT COMBINING WITH THE OTHER TWO TO PRODUCE A GLORIOUS SOUND.

PEAS AND PROSCIUTTO

SERVES 4-6

You can't get away from it. Classic recipes are classic for a reason. They taste good (sometimes marvelous), and although the ingredients may be commonplace, they somehow have an affinity that is instantly recognizable at the first bite. Peas and prosciutto ham fall into this category. This dish is essentially greens and fatback taken to the ultimate. Though it is a refined version, it still reaches your taste buds with all the vigor of its more humble cousin. This recipe calls for shelled peas, but you can substitute sugar snap peas, which are whole pods with fully developed peas inside, or sliced Chinese pea pods.

Heat olive oil in a large sauté pan and add garlic. Cook for one minute, stirring with a wooden spoon. Do not allow the garlic to darken, or it will taste bitter. Add the peas and stir well to coat. Add the dried thyme and cook another minute. Add the water. When liquid simmers, lower heat and cover. Cook for 5 or 6 minutes, or until peas are tender. Drain, then return mixture to the pan along with the parsley, butter, minced prosciutto, and salt and pepper to taste. Serve hot. This goes very well with fish, especially salmon.

TIP: YOU CAN OMIT THE PROSCIUTTO AND ADD 2 CUPS QUARTERED, STEAMED NEW POTATOES, 1 CUP COOKED, DRAINED BLACK BEANS, 1 TABLESPOON OLIVE OIL, AND 2 TABLESPOONS CHOPPED FRESH DILL OR FRESH CILANTRO TO THE ABOVE FOR A VERY SATISFYING VEGETARIAN ENTREE.

2 tablespoons extra virgin olive oil

2 cloves minced or pressed garlic

6 cups shelled peas (about 7 pounds before shelling)

1 tablespoon dried thyme

1/2 cup water

2 tablesoons chopped flat leaf parsley

1 tablespoon sweet butter

3 ounces minced prosciutto

salt and freshly ground pepper to taste

POTATO CHEESE PUFF

SERVES 8-10 , OR 6 FOR A PIG-OUT

12 medium boiling potatoes, washed, unpeeled

1 teaspoon salt

2 large Spanish, or other sweet onions, minced

1/2 cup butter, divided

2 teaspoons curry powder

2 1/2 cups grated white Cheddar cheese

1 1/4 cups milk

1 cup sliced scallions, white and green parts

1/4 teaspoon cayenne pepper (optional)

salt and freshly ground pepper to taste

4 eggs, beaten

I love potatoes. I love them boiled, mashed, fried, steamed, baked, and any other way you can make them. They can be served as an accompaniment to an entree, or they can be the main course. They greet gravy like a beloved friend, all absorbing, no questions asked. Or they can be very pristine and want only a bit of salt. This is a recipe that can be carried to a potluck, or eaten hunched over the stove because you can't stop that little peck of a taste you started with. Am I waxing too poetic? Never mind. Try this, and you'll see what I mean.

Place potatoes and salt in a 3 quart pot, cover with cold water, and boil until tender. Peel potatoes, put them through a ricer, and then mash them thoroughly. Heat oven to 375 degrees. While potatoes are boiling, sauté the minced onions in a large sauté pan with 2 tablespoons butter until they are wilted, not brown. Add curry powder and cook another minute to dissolve the powder. Using a 3 or 4 quart saucepan, combine the sautéed onions with the mashed potatoes, the remaining butter, grated cheese, milk, scallions, cayenne, and salt and pepper. Reheat slowly, stirring to avoid scorching. Remove from heat and fold in the beaten eggs. Place the mixture in a greased 3 or 4 quart casserole or soufflé dish and bake for 45 minutes or until the potatoes are puffy and brown.

TIP: TO PEEL HOT, COOKED POTATOES, PLACE THEM ON A CLEAN CLOTH AND HOLDING THEM WITH A FORK, USE A SHARP KNIFE TO PEEL OFF THE SKIN. WITH A LITTLE PRACTICE, THIS METHOD IS QUITE EFFICIENT. POTATOES COOKED UNPEELED ABSORB LESS WATER AND RETAIN MORE NUTRIENTS AND FLAVOR, BUT IF YOU PREFER TO PEEL THEM FIRST, BY ALL MEANS, DO. ALSO, PUSHING THEM THROUGH A RICER BEFORE YOU WHIP THEM AVOIDS LUMPY POTATOES, BUT IS NOT ABSOLUTELY NECESSARY. (RICERS CAN USUALLY BE FOUND IN ANY GOOD KITCHEN STORE, SUCH AS KITCHEN PORT AT KERRYTOWN. YOU COULD ALSO USE A FOLEY FOOD MILL.)

POTATO TURNIP PUREE

SERVES 6

This classic accompaniment to duck is good with any savory entrée. The strong flavor of the turnips is tempered by the potatoes and the result is subtle and delicious. Don't be tempted to cook the turnips and potatoes together, as the strong flavor of the turnips will take over!

2 pounds peeled turnips

2 pounds unpeeled potatoes

5 cloves peeled garlic

3 tablespoons sweet butter

3 tablespoons heavy cream

salt and freshly ground pepper to taste

Cut turnips into quarters and place them in a large saucepan with water to cover. Boil until soft. Strain turnips through a ricer, reserving some of the liquid in case you need to enhance the purée. Boil whole potatoes until soft, along with the garlic. Peel potatoes and push through a ricer, along with the garlic. Whip them in a mixer with strained turnips. Add butter, cream, and salt and pepper to taste. Be careful not to overwhip the mixture, as it will turn into a gluey mess. If you would prefer a stronger turnip taste, add a little of the reserved liquid in which the turnips were cooked.

TIP: This recipe can be made a day ahead and reheated.

TIP: Another bonus from the Farmers' Market! Save the turnip greens to steam with a little water, olive oil, garlic, salt and pepper. (Remove any tough stems and tear leaves into smaller pieces first.)

ROASTED HERBED VEGETABLES

1/2 cup extra virgin olive oil

1/4 cup Balsamic vinegar

1 tablespoon Dijon mustard

1 tablespoon fresh lemon juice

1 tablespoon fresh lime juice

1 tablespoon dried tarragon

1 tablespoon dried thyme

1 teaspoon salt

1/2 teaspoon freshly
ground pepper

2 medium bulbs fennel,
cut into 6 pieces each

1 yellow bell pepper,
cut into 8 pieces

1 red bell pepper,
cut into 8 pieces

2 Japanese eggplants, quartered

1 purple onion, outer skin
removed, cut into 8 pieces

1 sweet potato, scrubbed, skin on,
cut into 8 pieces

1 whole bulb garlic, top third
removed, skin left on

1 cup chopped mixed fresh herbs

1 cup toasted pine nuts
(see "Basics")

The end of summer at the Farmers' Market is a most glorious time. Months of hard work and careful planning result in a profusion of fruits and vegetables, and the eyes are dazzled. "Buy them all!" says the devil on your shoulder. "You'll find a way to eat them all. Go ahead, buy everything you see!" And so you do. When you get home, you feel pretty silly when you look at your thousand pounds of lovely stuff. Never fear. Roast them all, and eat them for a week. This recipe is relatively low in calories, supremely easy to prepare, and can be served as a first course, a party offering, or even as a main course. If you become desperate, you can even purée the last bits with a little chicken stock, milk or cream, for a tasty soup. Be sure to use a really good-tasting olive oil, and a variety of herbs.

Heat oven to 350 degrees. Make a vinaigrette by combining olive oil, Balsamic vinegar, mustard, lemon and lime juices, dried herbs, and salt and pepper in a large bowl. Whisk until emulsified and well blended. Or combine ingredients in a bottle with a tight lid, and shake until well mixed..

Place all of the remaining ingredients (except the fresh herbs and the toasted nuts)in a large bowl and pour the vinaigrette over them, carefully turning them over so all of the vegetables are well coated.

Transfer this mixture to a large shallow pan or oven-proof serving dish, arranging them attractively. Cover with waxed paper, or parchment paper, and then with aluminum foil. Roast for 30 minutes. Remove the foil and test vegetables for doneness with a sharp knife. If not done, replace foil and test again in 10 minutes.

Top with chopped fresh herbs and pine nuts, and serve either individual portions, or as part of a buffet. Separate the cloves from the bulb of garlic, and give each diner a few cloves to be squeezed out of their skins, onto the vegetables, or arrange the cloves on the serving platter. Serve with Olive Anchovy Paste (see "Embellishments").

TIP: OTHER DRIED AND FRESH HERBS AND OTHER VEGETABLES CAN BE SUBSTITUTED OR ADDED TO THE ABOVE. USE WHATEVER YOU HAVE. SCALLIONS AND ASPARAGUS ARE A DELICIOUS ADDITION. YOU CAN ALSO ROAST 2 OR 3 LEMONS, CUT INTO QUARTERS, ALONG WITH THE VEGETABLES.

SCALLOPED TOMATOES

SERVES 6

What is a "scalloped" anything? In the sense of this recipe, the word, which comes from the French, indicates something that is pounded thinly. It has also come to mean a dish of many thin things layered together. Tomatoes or potatoes lend themselves very nicely to this meaning, but there are other types of foods which, when bound in a creamy sauce and topped with bread crumbs, may also be called "scalloped" or "escalloped." This particular dish has always been a favorite of mine. Deceptively simple, uncommonly good. Bright red tomatoes sprinkled with Parmesan cheese, bread crumbs, herbs, and scallions are a perfect accompaniment to meat, fowl or seafood. Use firm, ripe tomatoes that won't disintegrate in cooking.

Heat oven to 350 degrees. Cut tomatoes in 1/2 inch slices. It is not necessary to peel the tomatoes, although you can if you prefer. (Plunge them into boiling water for 2 minutes, and then into iced water. The skins will peel off easily.) Layer the slices in a flat casserole dish that has been brushed with olive oil.

Place chopped scallions and parsley in the bowl of a food processor. Process briefly. Add minced garlic, Parmesan cheese, and bread crumbs and process for 5 seconds, just to mix evenly. Remove from bowl and add olive oil and hazelnuts. Sprinkle this mixture over the tomatoes. Heat in oven for 20 minutes. Serve hot or room temperature.

TIP: THIS MAKES A TERRIFIC MAIN COURSE IF YOU POUR THREE OR FOUR BEATEN EGGS OVER THE TOP AND COOK AS ABOVE. ADD 2 OR 3 DICED (CANNED) JALAPEÑO PEPPERS FOR SOME EXTRA ZING.

---

6 medium tomatoes

olive oil for brushing casserole dish

3 scallions, green and white parts, chopped

3 tablespoons chopped parsley

2 cloves garlic, minced

1/2-3/4 cup grated Parmesan Reggiano cheese

1/2 cup dry bread crumbs

2 tablespoons extra virgin olive oil

1/4 cup ground roasted hazelnuts (see "Basics")

salt and freshly ground pepper to taste

SPINACH AMBROSIA

SERVES 6

This is spinach brought to its most delectable heights. The secret is in the freshness of the spinach and the grating of fresh nutmeg which brings out its buttery, subtle flavor. From early spring, spinach appears already bagged and washed in the Farmers' Market.

Its flavor diminishes with time, so be prepared to eat it within a day or two. I steam it as soon as I can, and store it in the refrigerator until I am ready to use it. That way, it takes up less room and is ready to use when I need it.

Fill your kitchen sink with water, and have a large colander ready to use for draining. Trim off any tough stems of the spinach. Wash spinach in several changes of water, draining it well between each soaking. There's nothing worse than biting on a grain of dirt when you are savoring this dish. It is not necessary to dry the spinach. Heat oven to 325 degrees. Place washed and drained spinach in a 4 or 5 quart pot, add water and salt, and cover. Bring to a steaming boil, lower heat, and cook until spinach is wilted. This should take about 5 or 6 minutes. Immediately drain the spinach into a colander and plunge it into a large bowl of very cold water. This will set the color to a bright emerald green. Drain the cooked spinach very well, pressing out all the water with the palms of your hands, or placing it in a clean towel and wringing the towel with the spinach. Purée the spinach in the bowl of a food processor or blender until it is very fine. Add the garlic, béchamel sauce, grated nutmeg, and salt and pepper to taste.

Grease a shallow 1 quart casserole dish and pour in the spinach mixture. Place in preheated oven and cook for 20 minutes, or until the spinach is bubbling and heated through.

Tip: TOP THE SPINACH WITH 1/2-3/4 CUP GRATED PARMESAN REGGIANO CHEESE BEFORE BAKING IT, FOR AN ADDED BOOST OF FLAVOR.

Ingredients (sidebar):

3 bunches spinach (about 3 pounds), well washed and trimmed

1/2 cup water

1/2 teaspoon salt

3 cloves minced garlic

1 cup béchamel sauce (see "Sauces")

1/4 teaspoon grated nutmeg

salt and freshly ground pepper to taste

olive oil for brushing casserole dish

1/2-3/4 cup grated Parmesan Reggiano cheese (optional)

ST. CLAIR'S ESCALLOPED
BEANS & TOMATOES

=== SERVES 6 ===

Here is proof that simplicity is frequently the key to excellence. Louise St. Clair generously shares this family recipe, passed down from generation to generation as part of a holiday tradition. Whether you call it "escalloped" or "scalloped," it is a deceptively simple and remarkably delicious side dish.

Heat oven to 350 degrees. Butter a 6 cup casserole. Mix cracker or bread crumbs and butter together in a large bowl. Add the remaining ingredients, tossing together gently. Pour into greased baking dish. Arrange uncooked bacon slices on top and bake in oven for 25-30 minutes.

TIP: You can substitute canned tomatoes for the fresh ones.

1 cup cracker crumbs or dry bread crumbs

4 tablespoons melted butter (reserve some for greasing pan)

2 cups cooked fresh or frozen lima beans

1 1/2 cups fresh tomatoes, peeled and roughly chopped

1/2 teaspoon salt

1/4 teaspoon pepper

1/4 teaspoon celery salt

3 tablespoons chopped onion

4 slices uncooked bacon

DESSERTS

I used to think that if I served a spectacular first course and a rich dessert (usually something chocolate), my guests would be happy with the entire meal. But I have a passion for peaches, pears, apples, plums, and berries, and now I have come to believe that the simple, clean taste of ripe fruit is the perfect finish to a meal. What could be better than a fresh peach tart, bursting with the juices of summer? Or a strudel filled with the spring's first rhubarb? How about a warm apple cheese cake, or a prickly pear sorbet? By all means, follow the recipes, for fruit risotto, plum oat bars, and pears with chocolate sauce, among others. But also think of them as a loose outline for inventing your own dishes. Substitute one fruit for another, add or subtract an ingredient, or two, using your own palate as a guide. Have a good time!

APPLE TART WITH MONTEREY JACK CHEESE

=== SERVES 6-8 ===

For the crust:

1 1/2 cups all purpose flour

2 tablespoons sugar

1/4 teaspoon salt

6 tablespoons cold, sweet butter, cut into small pieces

1 egg, beaten

For the filling:

2 -2 1/2 cups tart apples, peeled, cored, and sliced

1 tablespoon lemon juice

2 tablespoons maple sugar

1 tablespoon granulated sugar

1 tablespoon flour

1 tablespoon cinnamon

2 tablespoons chopped, candied ginger (optional)

1/2 cup sugar

1/2 cup all purpose flour

3/4 cup grated Monterey Jack cheese

6 tablespoons sweet butter, cut into small pieces

Who doesn't like apple pie? And what is more American than a piece of apple pie with a hunk of cheese? This recipe uses grated Monterey Jack cheese as part of the baked topping to replace the usual cheese on the side. Use a tart apple, such as Winesap, Jonagold, or Granny Smith, which will hold up very well against the cheese. Use maple sugar if you can, but brown sugar may be substituted. Serve the pie warm, with (and why not?) vanilla ice cream.

Place flour, sugar, salt and butter in the bowl of a food processor. Process very briefly, until a coarse texture is attained. Add the beaten egg and process just until dough forms a ball. Press dough together, wrap in plastic wrap, or place in a plastic bag, and chill at least one hour.

Heat oven to 350 degrees. Roll out dough between two sheets of waxed paper or parchment paper, and line a 9 or 10 inch tart pan. Prick the bottom of the shell with a fork and proceed with the filling.

Combine the apple slices, lemon juice, two sugars, flour, cinnamon, and candied ginger. Fill the tart shell with this mixture. Mix together the 1/2 cup sugar, 1/2 cup flour and grated Monterey Jack cheese and sprinkle over the filling. Dot with butter and bake for 35-40 minutes.

APPLE BREAD PUDDING WITH WHISKEY SAUCE

SERVES 6-8

This recipe needs to be started at least 12 hours in advance. The secret is in the soaking of the ingredients to blend their textures and flavors. It's a great dessert to take to a tailgate party or a potluck, and its homespun simplicity makes it a real winner after a fancy dinner. Although the recipe calls for croissants, you can use any white bread or even brioche, a rich yeast bread that contains lots of butter and eggs. At this writing, Brewbakers is making brioche in its traditional hat-shaped form.)

At least 12 hours before you plan to serve the bread pudding tear the croissants or bread into rough chunks. Using a large bowl, combine the croissants or bread, diced apple, maple sugar, milk, raisins and dried apricots, and orange rind. Cover and place in refrigerator overnight, or for at least 12 hours. Heat oven to 350 degrees. Grease an 8"x 11" baking dish with melted butter or margarine. Combine the remaining ingredients in a small bowl and whisk them together until the eggs are thoroughly beaten. Pour this custard mixture into the soaked bread mixture. Pour the bread/custard mixture into the greased dish and bake for 1 hour or until puffy. Cool for about 5 minutes and pour the whiskey sauce over the top.

You can serve this with 2 cups heavy cream, whipped and sweetened with 2 tablespoons granulated sugar and 1 teaspoon vanilla.

---

8 large croissants, or 12 slices bread or brioche

2 Granny Smith or Jonagold apples, peeled and cut into 1 inch dice

3 tablespoons maple sugar

5 1/2 cups milk

3/4 cup golden raisins

1/2 cup diced dried apricots

1 tablespoon grated orange rind (see "Basics")

1 tablespoon butter or margarine, melted

4 large eggs

1 tablespoon vanilla extract

1 cup sugar

1/2 teaspoon grated nutmeg

1 tablespoon freshly grated ginger root

1 recipe Whiskey Sauce (see "Basics")

2 cups heavy cream, whipped (optional)

2 tablespoons granulated sugar (optional)

1 teaspoon vanilla (optional)

CHOCOLATE CHERRY CARDAMOM RICE PUDDING

=== SERVES 8-12 ===

1 cup sour cherries, pits removed

1/3 cup bourbon

2 tablespoons cardamom seeds

rind from one whole orange (white pith removed)

1 tablespoon sugar

3 ounces grated bittersweet chocolate

14 ounces sweetened condensed milk

2/3 cup whole milk

1 egg yolk and 1 whole egg

2 1/2 cups cooked medium or short grain white rice

1 package slightly thawed frozen raspberries, puréed and strained

1 recipe of custard (see "Basics")

This is one of those desserts that falls into the "Instant Nostalgia" category. To taste it once is to be addicted forever. The combination of the fragrant cardamom and the seductive taste of the bittersweet chocolate is a brilliant marriage of flavors.

Heat oven to 350 degrees. Soak the pitted cherries in bourbon about 10 minutes. Pulverize the cardamom seeds in a blender or food processor along with the orange peel and sugar. Combine mixture with the soaked cherries. Place the chocolate and condensed milk in the top of a double boiler and heat until chocolate is melted. Whisk together the milk, egg yolk and whole egg and add to the chocolate mixture. Add the cooked rice and the cherry mixture to the chocolate/egg mixture and combine. Pour the mixture into a 2 1/2 quart mold and place in a pan deep enough to hold boiling water poured half-way up the mold. Bake for 45 minutes, or until the pudding is set. The center of the pudding should be quite soft. Serve hot or warm in individual bowls with the puréed raspberries and custard sauce poured over the top.

TIP: SOUR CHERRIES ARE AVAILABLE MOST OF THE YEAR IN THE FROZEN FOOD SECTION OF SUPERMARKETS (AND, OF COURSE, FRESH DURING THE SUMMER). IF YOU CAN'T FIND THEM, SUBSTITUTE FRESH RASPBERRIES.

CITRUS DELIGHT

═══ SERVES 6-8 ═══

I couldn't resist including this recipe, even though citrus does not grow in Michigan. But plump, juicy navel oranges can be found in the middle of winter, and the rest of the ingredients are almost always available. The oranges at Zingerman's Practical Produce or the People's Food Co-op in the Kerrytown market are excellent, and since there are so few ingredients in this recipe, make sure they are premium. This recipe is easy, easy, easy to make. The star anise is the secret ingredient that lifts the dish above the ordinary. The slivers of orange peel are not cooked to the candied state.

1/2 cup granulated sugar

1 cup water

2 or 3 whole star anise pods

2 tablespoons (approximately) julienne of orange rind, white pith removed (see "Basics")

6-8 seedless navel oranges

8 kumquats, thinly sliced, seeds removed, skin left on

Using a 2 or 3 cup saucepan, combine the sugar, water, star anise, and julienne of orange rind. Bring mixture to a boil over medium heat and cook about 10 minutes until the sugar is completely dissolved and the orange rind is soft. Remove from heat and cool.

Remove the skin from the oranges in the following manner: Cut a thick slice from each end of the orange, right through to the flesh. Stand the orange on end and insert the knife between the skin and the flesh of the orange, removing the skin and the white pith in a downward stroke. Continue around the orange until all the skin is removed. When skin is completely removed, cut the orange in half. Lay the flat side of each half on a cutting board, and cut it into thirds. Make two slices across each third, and you will end up with bite-sized pieces of orange. Repeat with the other half and with the remaining oranges. Place orange pieces in a bowl large enough to hold them and pour the cooled sugar and star anise liquid over them. Do not strain the liquid. Cut each kumquat into thin slices across the short sides and add the slices to the oranges. Be sure to remove the seeds from the kumquats. Chill for at least one hour. Remove the star anise from the mixture before serving.

EASIEST TART IN THE WORLD

SERVES 6-8

1 sheet prepared puff pastry dough

1 egg yolk mixed with 2 tablespoons heavy cream (optional)

3 or 4 Granny Smith apples

about 1/2 cup sugar

1/2-3/4 cup strained apricot jam

2 tablespoons apricot liqueur, rum, cognac or orange juice

1 cup heavy cream (optional)

1 teaspoon vanilla (optional)

2 tablespoons sugar (optional)

I've named this the "Easiest Tart in the World" because it has always been my back-up for a last minute dessert, and I almost always have the ingredients on hand with which to make it. You can make it with purchased dough, or make your own puff-pastry from your favorite recipe. It is always devoured to the last crumb, and praise is always forthcoming. Be sure to use a baking pan with sides, like a jelly roll pan, to contain any hot butter which might exude from the dough.

Preheat oven to 400 degrees. Roll out dough on a lightly floured board until it is about 1/8" thick. You may leave the dough in the rectangular shape that you have rolled out, or using the bottom of a cake pan, trace and cut out a 9" circle, carefully trimming off the excess dough with a sharp knife. Place puff pastry on an ungreased baking sheet, and brush dough with the egg yolk/cream mixture. Prick the dough all over with a fork. Place in refrigerator while you cut the apples into slices.

Core, but do not peel the apples. Cut them into quarters, and slice each quarter in thin (about 1/4") slices. Remove dough from refrigerator and if you are using a rectangle, place the apple slices in an overlapping pattern in rows straight across the dough. If you are using a circle of dough, start at the outside edge, and form concentric circles, still overlapping the apple slices. Make sure the dough is covered to about 1/2" of each edge. Sprinkle about 1/2 cup sugar over the apples and place the tart in the oven. Heat until the apples are soft and the dough is light brown. This should take about 1/2 hour. If dough puffs too high, keep pricking it (through the apple slices).

While tart is cooking, warm about 1 cup apricot jam (covered) in the microwave for about 1 minute. Strain preserves and thin with a little liqueur or juice of your choice. Brush this over the tart while it is still warm. Serve warm with optional whipped cream, whipped only to a soft peak with the sugar and vanilla.

TIP: YOU MAY NEED MORE APPLES, DEPENDING ON THE SIZE APPLE YOU ARE USING. BE SURE TO HAVE ENOUGH ON HAND TO COMPLETE THE TART.

TIP: APRICOT GLAZE IS USED A GREAT DEAL IN BAKING, SO I WOULD ADVISE YOU TO STRAIN A WHOLE JAR OF PRESERVES AND KEEP IT ON HAND.

FRESH PEAR SOUFFLÉ

═ SERVES 6-8 ═

Michigan pears, which reach their peak in September, are the basis of this sumptuous dessert. The aroma of a fresh pear has always been very enticing to me. If you can keep from eating them while you are preparing this, you're a better person than I am. Fortunately, the market provides a plentiful amount, and there's always enough for me and my soufflé. This recipe is a take-off on one served at a well-known 3 star restaurant in Paris. It calls for an eau-de-vie of pear, which is a very aromatic pear brandy. If you can't find it, use any other clear fruit brandy.

Combine 1 1/4 cups of the sugar and the water in a 2 to 3 quart saucepan. Bring to a simmer and cook over low heat until the sugar dissolves, stirring with a wooden spoon from time to time.

Peel, quarter, and core the pears. Add them to the syrup and cook until they are tender, about another 20 minutes. The pears should be covered with liquid as they cook, so add more water if necessary. Drain the pears, and cut half of them into small dice. Butter 8 or 9 individual soufflé molds and dust them with 1/4 cup of the sugar. Distribute the diced pears among the molds. Heat oven to 475 degrees. Puree the remaining pears and return to the pan, along with the grated ginger. When the purée is reduced to about 2 cups, remove it from heat and keep at room temperature.

Dissolve the remaining 1 cup sugar in 1/3 cup of water and cook it over medium heat until it reaches the hard crack stage (300 degrees on a candy thermometer). Do not stir the syrup once the sugar has dissolved. Pour the hot syrup over the warm pear purée. Stir this mixture, then add the pear eau-de-vie.

Beat the egg whites until they hold soft peaks. Fold the pear mixture and egg whites together and distribute the mixture among the 8 or 9 soufflé molds. Place in preheated oven and bake for 10 minutes, or until the soufflés are puffy and brown.

2 1/2 cups granulated sugar, separated

3 cups water

8-10 very ripe pears

1 tablespoon grated fresh ginger

1/3 cup water

5 tablespoons pear eau-de-vie

8 or 9 large egg whites

FRESH WHITE PEACH TART

1 recipe of Sweet Tart Dough
(see "Basics")

1/4 cup granulated sugar

4 cups white wine

1/2 cup water

4 or 5 strips of orange peel

1 teaspoon vanilla

8 medium to large, firm peaches,
whole, unpeeled

1/2 cup unsalted butter, room
temperature

6 ounces almond paste

1/2 cup confectionery sugar

1/2 cup all purpose flour

3/4 cup ground almonds

2 tablespoons grated orange rind

5 egg whites

1/2 cup apricot jam, warmed
with 1 tablespoon rum

Farmers' Market customers are fortunate to be able to buy produce in its ripe stage. If you are lucky enough to be there when the Kapnicks or the Nemeths have their white peaches on hand, be sure to try them. Since they are fragile and bruise easily, really good white peaches can hardly ever be found outside local markets. When they are picked ripe, their delicate flavor and lush ripeness cannot be matched. In commercial markets, because they are picked underripe to be shipped, white peaches never seem to attain that same degree of delectability. This recipe is a supreme use of fresh peaches. The dough is short and sweet, and the almond filling enhances the natural luscious flavor of the peach.

Prepare one recipe of sweet tart dough (see "Basics"). Heat oven to 375 degrees. Bake the tart shell for 5-7 minutes, until done but not brown. Cool before filling. Combine the granulated sugar, white wine, and water in a 4 or 5 quart saucepan along with the orange peel and vanilla. Bring the mixture to a boil and add the whole peaches. Simmer for 8 minutes. The skins will begin to loosen. Using a slotted spoon, remove the peaches from the liquid and plunge them into a large bowl of very cold water. The skins will slip off. Drain them and proceed with recipe.

Combine the softened butter and the almond paste and beat until the mixture is well combined and somewhat creamy. Add the confectionery sugar, all-purpose flour, ground almonds, and orange rind and beat until well combined. Beat egg whites until they are soft and foamy. Combine with the almond paste mixture. Spread this blend evenly into the baked tart shell. Cut the peaches into quarters, or slices, and arrange them in a decorative pattern over the filling. Bake for 45 to 50 minutes, or until the filling is set. Strain the warm apricot jam/rum mixture, then brush it over the top of tart. Serve at room temperature or warm.

TIP: IF WHITE PEACHES ARE NOT AVAILABLE, YOU CAN SUBSTITUTE NECTARINES OR YELLOW PEACHES.

FRUIT RISOTTO

═══ SERVES 6 ═══

Three cheers for comfort food! This combination of rum-soaked peaches, golden raisins, and cherries is added to rice that has been cooked with ginger-flavored milk. It is best eaten warm or at room temperature. Although the name "risotto" usually implies that the grains of rice have a firm center when the cooking is completed, it is the creaminess of the fully cooked short grain rice that gives character to this dish. We cook the rice in the conventional manner rather than the classic Italian way, which would add the liquid little by little. The final result will have a soft texture, enhanced by the aroma and chewiness of the fruits.

Soak the diced peaches, raisins, and cherries in the dark rum for at least 30 minutes. Melt the butter in a heavy 2 quart saucepan. Add the rice, mixing well to coat the grains with the butter. Add the hot milk, grated ginger, sugar, and ground cardamom to the pan. Cover, lower heat, and cook rice for 20 minutes. Take off heat and let stand, covered, to steam the rice for another 5 minutes. Remove cover (watch out for steam), add the drained rum-soaked fruits, and the chopped candied ginger. Mix well. Spoon into individual serving bowls and serve with custard flavored with the optional rum.

1 cup peeled and diced fresh peaches

1/2 cup golden raisins

1 cup pitted fresh or frozen (thawed) cherries

1/2 cup dark rum

2 tablespoons butter

1 cup short grain rice, preferably Arborio

2 cups hot milk

1 tablespoon grated fresh ginger

2 tablespoons granulated sugar

1/2 teaspoon ground cardamom

1/4 cup chopped candied ginger

1 recipe custard (see "Basics")

2 tablespoons rum (optional)

GRANDMA'S SHORTBREAD

═══ YIELD: 8-10 SLICES ═══

1/2 cup cornstarch

1 1/2 cups flour

1/4 cup confectionery sugar

1/4 cup granulated sugar

1/2 pound softened butter

Shortbread is generally associated with Christmas and Scotland, and its rich buttery goodness is loved by all of us self-indugent food lovers. It's traditional round shape stems from being pressed into a molded griddle, with notched edges signifying the rays of the sun. Mike Potter of Hill O' Beans Coffee and Smiling Cat Tea Merchants at the indoor Kerrytown Market loves this tasty shortbread recipe and suggests having it with a fragrant cup of tea.

Preheat oven to 325 degrees. Sift flour and cornstarch together.

Cream butter, confectionery and granulated sugar together, and blend into the sifted mixture. Press into a pie pan, or a 9 inch springform pan, and bake for 1 hour, or until light brown. Loosen with a knife around the edge to remove. Sprinkle top with granulated sugar, if desired.

TIP: SCORING THE UNBAKED SHORTBREAD INTO 8 OR 10 SLICES BEFORE YOU BAKE IT, WILL FACILITATE CUTTING THE SLICES AFTER BAKING.

JAN KAPNICK'S FRESH PEACH PIE

Here is a perfect example of less is more. Just fill a baked pie shell with luscious, perfectly ripe peaches, top with a glaze, and you have a dish that sings of summer. The fragrance and taste of homegrown peaches cannot be matched by the store-bought fruit. It is simply not possible to pick, pack, and ship fully ripe peaches, as they are too fragile, and prone to bruising. This means that they must be picked before they are ripe. While it is true that peaches will further ripen off the tree, the result in the store is not quite the same as that fully ripened, freshly plucked peach from the Farmers' Market. What a treat!

Dissolve the cornstarch in the water. Add the gelatin, sugar, and almond extract. Bring the mixture to a boil in a 4 cup pot and cook for one minute. Cool about 30 minutes and then mix with the sliced peaches. Pour into baked pie shell and cool for 3 or 4 hours before serving. Top with whipped cream or whipped topping.

1 baked 9 inch pie shell

2 tablespoons cornstarch

1 cup cold water

1 package peach gelatin

1 cup granulated sugar

1/4 teaspoon almond extract

6 cups sliced, peeled, fresh peaches

2 cups whipped cream or whipped topping (optional)

KITCHEN PORT'S CHOCOLATE BABKA

=YIELD: 1 FOURTEEN INCH LOAF PAN=

Babka is of Polish origin. The word usually refers to a yeast bread studded with fruits and nuts, and sometimes with rum flavoring. This version, from Kitchen Port's Connie Rosenthal, is made in a loaf pan, with a chocolate almond filling and is sprinkled with a cardamom-scented streusel. Sounds wonderful and it is. Sit yourself down in the middle of the afternoon, and have a thick slice of warm babka and a cup of good tea or coffee, and maybe, maybe, invite a friend (a good one), and you will be renewed, revivified, re-energized. This recipe is divided into three parts: the dough, the filling, and the topping. It's not complicated, but do read it through first, as you should with all recipes.

For the dough:

1 tablespoon granular (dry) yeast

1/3 cup warm water
(about 115-120 degrees)

3 1/4 cups bread flour

1 1/2 teaspoons salt

3 tablespoons sugar

3 tablespoons non-fat dry milk

8 ounces sweet butter,
melted and cooled

1 tablespoon vegetable oil,
or oil spray

For the filling:

6 ounces semisweet chocolate,
chopped

2 egg whites

17 ounce tube of almond paste

For the topping:

1/2 cup soft sweet butter

1/2 cup brown sugar

1/2 cup all purpose flour

1 teaspoon ground cardamom

For the dough:

Dissolve yeast in water. Combine flour, salt, sugar, and non-fat dry milk in a large bowl. Add dissolved yeast and melted butter to the flour mixture and knead with a dough hook or by hand until smooth. Place dough in a large bowl greased with vegetable oil or spray. Cover with plastic wrap and refrigerate overnight or as long as 48 hours.

For the filling:

Combine all of these ingredients in a food processor until well blended. Remove to a small bowl.

For the topping:

Combine all of these ingredients in a food processor until well blended. Remove to bowl.

To construct and bake the babka:

Heat oven to 350 degrees. Roll out dough in a 10 inch x 14 inch rectangle. Spread with chocolate filling. Sprinkle 2/3 of the streusel topping over the chocolate filling, and roll up the dough jelly-roll fashion. Place in loaf pan and sprinkle the top with the remainder of streusel. Let rise, covered, for 45 minutes. Bake for 30-40 minutes. Cool to room temperature before serving.

LOUETTA DIETERLE'S CINNAMON STARS

=== YIELD: 4 DOZEN ===

Walking into Bob and Louetta Dieterle's tidy and welcoming kitchen, one gets the feeling that good things happen here. The cribbage board is ready and the stove is spotless. This is a good, old-fashioned cookie recipe, and just like the good, old-fashioned dahlias we purchase at their market stand, it inspires our confidence for its integrity and quality. And these taste good, too! Do not be confused by the lack of flour as the ground nuts take its place.

Beat egg whites until stiff. Add sugar and beat 15 minutes. Remove and save 3/4 cup of this beaten mixture to use as frosting. Add ground nuts, cinnamon, and baking powder to the remaining egg white-sugar mixture. Cover the frosting and the dough separately with plastic wrap and refrigerate overnight. Heat oven to 300 degrees. Sprinkle counter with an equal mixture of cake flour and confectionery sugar and roll dough 1/4 inch thick. Spray vegetable oil on a baking sheet. Cut star shapes from the dough, place cookies on the baking sheet 2 inches apart, and frost cookies with the reserved beaten egg white/sugar mixture. Bake for 8-10 minutes. Check at 6 minutes to make sure they are not burning.

TIP: BE SURE TO REFRIGERATE THE BATTER OVERNIGHT, AS THIS ALLOWS THE SUGAR AND EGG WHITES TO STIFFEN.

6 egg whites

1 pound confectionery sugar

1/2 pound almonds, finely ground

1/2 pound English walnuts, finely ground

1 teaspoon cinnamon

1/2 teaspoon baking powder

cake flour and confectionery sugar to roll out the dough

NEMETHS' EASY CARROT PEAR BUNDT CAKE

4 eggs

1 1/2 cups granulated sugar

3/4 cup vegetable oil

1 teaspoon pure vanilla extract

2 cups unsifted all purpose flour

2 teaspoons baking soda

2 teaspoons baking powder

2 teaspoons cinnamon

1/4 teaspoon nutmeg

4 medium carrots, peeled and finely shredded (about 1 1/2 cups)

2 medium sized pears, peeled, pared, cored, and puréed

3/4 cup raisins

3/4 cup chopped walnuts

1 tablespoon vegetable oil

We need to have recipes in our repertoire that are dependable, delicious, and easy to make. This fits the bill. It's as dependable as the flavorful produce we purchase from the Nemeths at the Ann Arbor Farmers' Market. Have a cup of good coffee or tea ready, and share this treat with someone. The sweetness of the carrots plays off nicely against the subtle pear flavor. Once again, I realize how lucky we are to be able to buy produce that is grown in the area and that travels from the grower directly to the buyer. Purée the pears in a food processor or blender.

Heat oven to 350 degrees. In a large mixer bowl, beat together the eggs, sugar, vegetable oil, and vanilla until smooth. Combine the flour, baking soda, baking powder, cinnamon, and nutmeg. Add the dry ingredients alternately with the shredded carrots and puréed pears. Fold in the raisins and nuts. Grease a 9 inch bundt or tube pan with 1 tablespoon vegetable oil and flour the inside of the pan. Spoon the batter into the pan. Bake about 40 to 45 minutes or until cake springs back when touched lightly with the fingertips. Invert cake onto a rack and let cool for 10 minutes. Remove pan and sprinkle with confectionery sugar if desired.

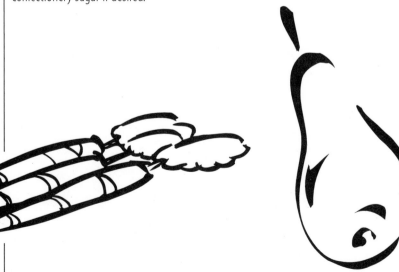

PEARS MAXINE

SERVES 6

Here is a version of an old favorite called Pears Helen. This new version is named in honor of the Market Master, Maxine Rosasco, who has been so generous with her time and information.

Pears are first poached in a light syrup flavored with star anise. Then they are stuffed with fresh raspberries and glazed with a hot chocolate hazelnut sauce. This is a wonderful dessert to make when pears are ripe, but not mushy, and raspberries are at their peak. Be sure to crush some of the raspberries so their full flavor will seep into the other ingredients. Star anise is a brown, star-shaped pod that is native to China, and although it is related to the magnolia family, it comes from an evergreen tree. Its anise flavor comes from anethol, an oil, which gives it a slightly bitter flavor.

In a pot large enough to hold the pears in a single layer, dissolve the sugar and water over low heat. When sugar is completely dissolved, add the vanilla and star anise. Cook for 5 minutes over low heat. Peel each pear and scoop out the core from the bottom with the end of a vegetable peeler. Be careful not to break apart the pear. Rub each pear all over with the cut ends of the lemon, squeezing some of the lemon juice over each pear. (This will help prevent the pears from discoloring.) Add the pears to the simmering poaching liquid. Keep them submerged by placing a pot lid directly on top of the pears. Cook for 5 minutes, or until the pears are slightly softened. Be careful not to overcook them, as they will become mushy. Drain the hot liquid, then remove the pears from the pot. (Alternatively, you can place the whole pot, pears, liquid, and all, in a sink full of cold water to stop the cooking.) Crush 1/3 of the raspberries and combine them with some of the remaining berries and the warm currant jelly. Reserve some berries, rolled separately in the currant jelly, for garnish. Spoon some of the currant jelly/berry mixture into the cored pears. Combine the ground hazelnuts with the warm chocolate sauce. Stand each pear in an individual serving dish and spoon some of the warm hazelnut chocolate sauce over the top. Decorate the bottom perimeter of each pear with some of the whipped cream flavored with rum and garnish with the remaining whole raspberries.

TIP: A LITTLE SOFTENED VANILLA ICE CREAM PLACED UNDER EACH POACHED STUFFED PEAR IS A SUBLIME ADDITION TO THIS DESSERT.

---

1 1/2 cups granulated sugar

3 cups water

1/2 teaspoon pure vanilla extract

6 star anise (available at Asian markets)

6 medium-sized Bartlett pears, peeled, left whole, stems on

1 lemon, cut in half

1 pint fresh raspberries

1/2 cup warm currant jelly

1 cup warm chocolate sauce (see "Sauces")

1/4 cup roasted hazelnuts, chopped fine (see "Basics")

1 cup heavy cream, whipped with 1 tablespoon sugar

1 tablespoon rum (optional)

PLUM OAT BARS

YIELD: 3 TO 4 DOZEN

1/3 cup light brown sugar

1 cup all-purpose flour

1 1/2 cups quick rolled oats

3/4 cup margarine

1 teaspoon lemon zest

1 teaspoon cinnamon

1/2 teaspoon nutmeg

1/4 teaspoon baking powder

1 1/2 cups chopped fresh plums mixed with 2 tablespoons sugar

Plums originated in Asia, and were then introduced into Europe by the Crusaders. After several millenia some varieties eventually found their way to the Wasem Fruit Farm and this quick recipe has been very popular with their customers.

These bars are a zip to make, and the tartness of the plums is an exquisite counterpoint to the oat mixture that supports them.

They keep very well, but probably will disappear as quickly as you make them.

Heat oven to 375 degrees. Combine all of the ingredients except plums. Pat this mixture into the bottom of a greased 9 inch square pan. Bake for 10 minutes. Remove from oven and cover with chopped plums which have been mixed with 2 tablespoons sugar. Bake another 20 minutes, or until golden brown. Cool and cut into bars.

PRICKLY PEAR SORBET

=== YIELD: ABOUT 4 SERVINGS ===

Years ago, when I was doing one of a few things I was entrusted to do in the kitchen of a 3-star restaurant in southern France, (how's that for name-dropping?), I was jolted out of my very important job of de-stemming a case of parsley to see the huge ice cream/sorbet machine being pulled out to the middle of the kitchen. What was the commotion? "Figues de Barbarie! Figues de Barbarie!" What the heck was that? So exotic sounding, so esoteric sounding, so elegant sounding! I quickly determined that figues de Barbarie were prickly pears, (sometimes called "cactus pear"), the fruit of several different kinds of cactus. Their shape is pear-like, and their flavor is sweet and a little bland. The skin is greenish-brown, the flesh can range from yellowish-green to deep purple, and there are black seeds scattered throughout which must be strained out before eating. It has an aroma a little like a melon. Choose ones that give slightly when pressed.

6 prickly pears, peeled

1 tablespoon fresh lemon juice

1 tablespoon vodka (optional)

1 cup granulated sugar

Peel prickly pears, and purée them in a food processor. Strain fruit through a sieve, or mesh strainer. You should have about 1 1/4 cups of fruit. Combine fruit with the remaining ingredients, and stir to help dissolve the sugar. Chill in refrigerator for at least 3 hours. Freeze the mixture in an ice cream freezer according to instructions.

Tip: IF YOU PREFER NOT TO USE VODKA, SUBSTITUTE 1 TABLESPOON OF FRUIT SYRUP, SUCH AS BLACKBERRY OR RASPBERRY.

RHUBARB STRUDEL

2 pounds rhubarb

1 cup raisins

1 cup granulated sugar, divided

1/2 teaspoon cinnamon

1/2 cup butter, melted

8 sheets filo dough

1 cup white bread crumbs

1 cup roasted chopped pecans (see "Basics")

2 cups sour cream, créme frâiche, (see "Basics"), or whipped cream

Among the first vegetables to appear in the spring is rhubarb, a member of the buckwheat family. Its stalks, which can attain up to 2 feet in height, resemble celery, and its leaves are poisonous. Choose crisp stalks that are brightly hued. Because it is tart, rhubarb is very often paired with fruit, such as strawberries or apples, and it usually needs quite a bit of sugar to tame it. It makes a great accompaniment to roast meats, and it is frequently baked into pies or tarts. Here is an easy strudel recipe that uses prepared filo dough. Topped with sour cream, créme frâiche, or loosely whipped heavy cream spiked with brandy, it is sublime.

Prepare the rhubarb by peeling any tough strands and cutting off the tough ends. Cut into 1 inch pieces and, using a large saucepan, combine rhubarb with 1/4 cup raisins, 1/4 cup sugar and cinnamon. Place over medium heat and cook for about 15 minutes. Cool to room temperature and proceed with recipe.

Melt butter in a small saucepan. Combine the remaining 3/4 cup sugar, the bread crumbs, and chopped roasted pecans in a food processor or blender, and process to a coarse consistency. Divide mixture into 8 portions.

Separate 1 sheet of filo dough and brush with some of the melted butter. Sprinkle one portion of the bread crumb mixture over the buttered sheet of dough. Divide the rhubarb mixture into 8 portions. Place one portion along the bottom third of the prepared dough sheet, using the short edge of the filo dough as the bottom edge. Fold in the two long edges of the filo dough toward the center, about 2 inches on each side, and roll the sheet from the bottom edge up to form a tight cylinder about 2 inches in diameter. Repeat with the remaining seven more sheets of dough, bread crumbs, and filling. Place the completed filo dough packages on a baking sheet lined with parchment or waxed paper, brush them with the remaining butter, and bake about 20 minutes, or until golden brown. Let the strudels sit for five minutes before serving. With a sharp knife, slice them across the middle at an angle, and serve topped with sour cream, créme frâiche, or whipped cream.

TIP: THIS STRUDEL IS ALSO DELICIOUS TOPPED WITH BERRIES AND A SCOOP OF VANILLA ICE CREAM.

SUMMER BERRY PUDDING

SERVES 6-8

This fresh berry pudding is usually made with slices of white bread, crusts trimmed off. It can also be put together with slices of angel food cake or even sponge cake. Try it the traditional way first. It has a lovely color and when served with flavored whipped cream it is a regal finish to any meal.

Use the bread to line the bottom and sides of a 2 quart mold, making sure to cover the entire surface. Overlap the slices of bread to form an interesting pattern.

Heat berries, sugar, ginger, and lemon rind over medium heat in a 3 quart saucepan for 5 minutes.

Use a slotted spoon to transfer berries to the bread-lined mold. Pour in the juice and cover contents with a round of parchment or waxed paper. Place a plate over the mold inside the perimeter of the waxed paper. Put a three pound weight on top of the plate, making sure to cover the entire plate. Chill pudding at least 12 hours, preferably 24.

When you are ready to serve the pudding, remove the weight and plate and run a spatula around the edges of the pudding to loosen it a bit. Place a large, chilled serving plate over the mold and invert the pudding onto the plate. Be sure to use a plate with raised sides, so juices do not spill off. Garnish with flavored whipped cream and whole berries.

TIP: ADDING A CUP OF CURRANTS TO THE BERRY MIXTURE MAKES A DELICIOUS VARIATION.

2 quart mold (any 2 quart bowl will do)

24 slices plain white bread, crusts removed

2 quarts fresh berries of choice, stems and hulls removed

2/3 cup granulated sugar

1 tablespoon grated ginger

1 teaspoon grated lemon rind

WASEM FRUIT FARM APPLE CHEESE CAKE

1 cup all-purpose flour

1 scant cup granulated sugar, divided

1/2 cup margarine (or butter)

3/4 teaspoon vanilla, divided

8 ounces softened cream cheese

1 beaten egg

1/2 teaspoon cinnamon

4 cups peeled and sliced
 baking apples
(Jonathan, Northern Red, Spy)

Apples are an ancient fruit and some scientific evidence shows that the first apples may have been the result of cross-breeding the Asian and the European crabapple, both of which still exist in their original species today. Early Greek and Roman poets and writers, mention apples. In 1695 the first orchard was planted in the new American colonies. Apples were an important crop for the colonist as they not only provided fresh fruit, but they dried well, could be stored over the winter, and were the basics for apple butter, apple sauce, cider, and cider vinegar.

"A" is for apple and "L" is for luscious, and that's what the following recipe is. In 1872 there were 1000 varieties of apples listed as being grown in America, compared with about 100 today. Leola Wasem grows 24 of the most popular varieties of apples and here is one of her personal recipe choices.

Heat oven to 425 degrees. Combine the flour and 1/3 cup of the sugar in a small bowl or in the bowl of a mixer. Add margarine, cut into small pieces and mix with a pastry cutter, or with the flat-sided tool of your electric mixer. Add 1/4 teaspoon vanilla and mix only until pea-sized lumps are formed. Do not overmix, or dough will be tough. Pat dough into the bottom of a 9 inch pie pan.

Soften the cream cheese with 1/4 cup sugar and 1 beaten egg. Add remaining 1/2 teaspoon vanilla. Spoon mixture onto the unbaked pie crust and spread it evenly.

Combine the remaining sugar, cinnamon, and sliced apples in a large bowl and mix gently. Arrange the apple slices in a decorative pattern over the cream cheese mixture. You will have more than one layer of apples.

Place pie on a baking sheet and place in preheated oven. Bake for 10 minutes, then reduce heat to 375 degrees. Continue to bake for 25 minutes. Cool and refrigerate. Serve at room temperature.

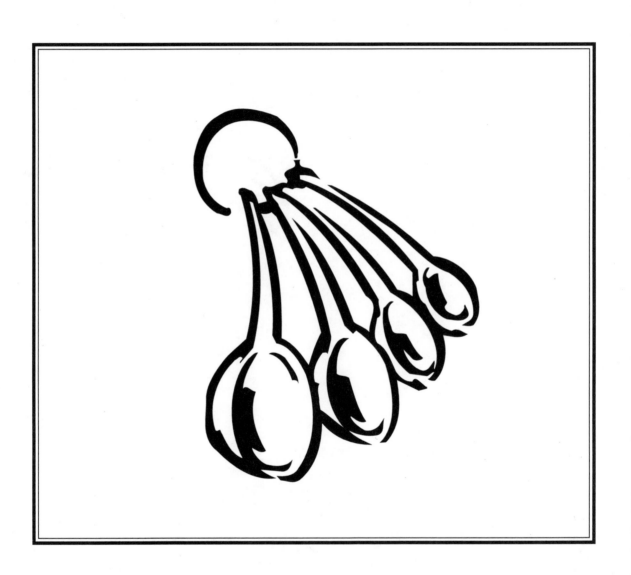

SAUCES

The final touch, sometimes simple, sometimes complex, always appreciated. Here, among others, is a juniper Port wine sauce for duck breasts, a chocolate sauce for pears, a roasted red pepper sauce for crab, a Gorgonzola sauce for gnocchi, a whiskey sauce for apple bread pudding. Try doubling the recipe, as I often do when I am making a sauce. Sauces usually freeze well, and are easily retrieved to turn an impromptu meal into an occasion, a good meal into a great one. The red wine sauce is marvelous on an omelet, for instance, and with some added chicken or veal stock, the roasted onion sauce can become a soothing soup. Think "sauce," think "innovate."

BÉCHAMEL OR WHITE SAUCE

YIELD: ABOUT 2 CUPS

5 tablespoons butter

4 tablespoons flour

2 cups warm milk, cream, stock, or a mixture of liquids

3/4 teaspoon salt and freshly ground pepper to taste

This is another backbone of good cooking. It can be made thick or thin, depending on what it is accompanying. The liquid is usually milk or cream, but any stock can be substituted for part of the liquid as a compatible flavoring.

Melt butter in a 1 quart saucepan over medium heat. Blend in the flour with a wooden spoon, mixing well. When mixture begins to bubble, add the warm liquid, about 1/2 cup at a time, whisking well during and after each addition. Increase the heat and continue to cook the mixture until it thickens. Add salt and pepper and remove from heat. Pour sauce through a sieve and cool.

TIP: FOR A THINNER SAUCE, REDUCE FLOUR TO 3 TABLESPOONS AND ADD 1/2 CUP LIQUID.

TIP: IF YOU WOULD LIKE TO ADD HERBS TO THIS SAUCE, A GOOD RULE OF THUMB IS TO ADD 2 TABLESPOONS OF THE FRESH LEAF AND 1/2 TEASPOON OF THE SAME HERB, DRIED. (FOR EXAMPLE, 2 TABLESPOONS OF CHOPPED FRESH BASIL AND 1/2 TEASPOON OF DRIED BASIL.) ADD MORE OR LESS, ACCORDING TO YOUR TASTE.

CHOCOLATE SAUCE

Who among us has never said "Just a little more chocolate sauce, please"? We chocoholics try to curb our greed, but the truth will out: It's never enough. This sauce can be enhanced by the addition of toasted ground nuts and brandy or rum, if desired. Be sure not to use unsweetened chocolate, sometimes called baking chocolate. The bittersweet chocolate called for here has been combined with some sugar, vanilla, and sometimes lecithin, which is a smoothing agent.

10 ounces dark semi-sweet or bittersweet chocolate

1 tablespoon butter

3/4 cup water

3/4 cup whipping cream

2 tablespoons rum, brandy, or liqueur of your choice

Grate chocolate or break into small pieces. Melt in the top of a double boiler, along with the butter, water, and cream. Add rum or brandy. Keep warm until ready to serve.

TIP: YOU MAY COMBINE ALL THE INGREDIENTS AND MELT THEM IN A MICROWAVE IN 30 SECOND INTERVALS AT THE HIGH SETTING. STIR AFTER 1 MINUTE TO COMBINE THE INGREDIENTS AND TEST FOR SMOOTHNESS.

CUSTARD SAUCE

4 egg yolks

1/3 cup sugar

1 1/2 cups milk

2 tablespoons flour

1 teaspoon pure vanilla extract

This is a light, pourable custard, sometimes called "créme Anglaise," or English pastry cream. It can be flavored with vanilla, instead of Kirsch, or any other liqueur, and it dresses up a pudding in a very elegant way.

Combine egg yolks with sugar in a mixing bowl. Beat until frothy. In a 1 quart saucepan mix 1/2 cup of the milk with the 2 tablespoons flour and stir until flour is dissolved. Add the rest of the milk and heat, stirring until slightly thickened. Pour a little of the hot milk into the beaten egg mixture, stirring to combine well and temper the mixture so the egg yolks will not curdle. Pour this mixture into the milk, and continue to cook until custard thickens. Keep the heat low and stir continuously. When the custard has the consistency of a thick milk shake and coats the spoon, remove from heat, and strain while it is still hot. Add vanilla and cover with plastic wrap.

TIP: THIS CUSTARD FREEZES VERY WELL.

FRESH TOMATO SAUCE

This recipe tastes best when made with fresh tomatoes, but it can also be concocted in the dead of winter, when the taste of a fresh tomato bears no relationship to its happy summer counterpart. In winter, use canned tomatoes. This is a simple, uncomplicated sauce. It can be dressed up, if you wish, with Balsamic vinegar, a tablespoon or so, to taste.

Peel the tomatoes by placing them in a large pot of boiling water, a few at a time, and then in a large bowl of iced water. The skins will slip right off. Remove stem ends of tomatoes and cut them in half. Squeeze over a strainer to remove seeds, retaining any juice which exudes. Cut tomatoes into large dice and place, along with their juice, in a 2 quart non-reactive saucepan. Because the acid in tomatoes causes aluminum to discolor and taints the sauce, and because ingesting aluminum is not good for you, use a stainless steel, porcelain, or anodyzed aluminum pan. Cook for about 10 minutes over low heat. Whisk in the butter, along with salt and pepper. Add the optional cream. Serve hot.

4 pounds very ripe Roma or plum tomatoes, seeded

3 tablespoons unsalted butter, cut into cubes

salt and freshly ground pepper

GORGONZOLA SAUCE

YIELD: ABOUT 1 1/2 CUPS

6 ounces Gorgonzola cheese

1/2 cup milk

4 tablespoons butter

1/2 cup heavy cream

1/2 cup freshly grated Parmesan Reggiano cheese

Gorgonzola cheese is an Italian blue-veined cheese, very salty and pungent. This aromatic sauce is for the hardy cheese lover. It is especially good with pasta or gnocchi.

In a shallow sauté pan, heat the milk, butter, and cheese. Whisk the sauce until the cheese becomes well incorporated. Stir in the heavy cream. When using wih gnocchi or pasta, pour some of the sauce onto the gnocchi or pasta as you remove each well-drained batch. Sprinkle on the Parmesan cheese at the end. One cup of cooked green peas can be added to the gnocchi or pasta at this point, as well as 1/2 cup chopped scallions.

TIP: IF SAUCE IS NOT THICK ENOUGH, MIX 2 TABLESPOONS CORNSTARCH WITH SOME COLD MILK AND ADD IT TO THE FINISHED SAUCE, COOKING IT ANOTHER 5 MINUTES, OR UNTIL IT THICKENS.

JUNIPER PORT WINE SAUCE

Remember all those black berries hanging from your juniper bushes? These are similar ones, only they are cultivated especially to eat, and they impart a pungent flavor to this sauce, which is mellowed by the smooth flavor of the wine. Juniper berries are also used to flavor gin, and are actually too bitter to eat raw, but when they are dried for commercial use are just right for sauce. Using clarified butter rather than just melted butter keeps the fat from burning; but if you prefer, you can substitute canola oil for the butter.

Using a 2 quart saucepan, sauté garlic and shallots in vegetable oil. Add red wine and reduce by half. Add Port and juniper berries and simmer for 5 minutes. Remove from heat, strain, and reserve.

Heat the clarified butter in a 1 quart saucepan. Add 1/4 cup flour and stir with a wooden spoon. Cook for a few minutes to get rid of the raw flour taste. Pour a little of the hot wine reduction into this butter/flour mixture (sometimes called a "roux") and stir or whisk. Whisk in remaining hot wine reduction. Keep saucepan over low heat, being careful not to let the mixture burn. At this point, add any deglazed juices from the pan in which you have seared the entrée meat, such as duck breasts.

1 tablespoon vegetable oil

2 cloves garlic, minced

4 large shallots, chopped

4 cups red wine

1/4-1/3 cup Port

1 teaspoon commercially dried juniper berries, crushed

1 cup concentrated beef (see Boiled Beef Dinner in "Entrees"), chicken or duck stock (see "Soups")

5 tablespoons clarified butter (see "Basics")

1/4 cup flour

salt and freshly ground pepper to taste

PESTO SAUCE

3 cups fresh basil,
stems and leaves

4 tablespoon pine nuts, walnuts,
or hazelnuts

4 cloves garlic, peeled

1 teaspoon salt

3/4 cup freshly grated Parmesan
Reggiano cheese

3/4 cup extra virgin olive oil

This classic uncooked sauce can be made during the summer when fresh basil is perfuming the air at the market. Use it on plain pasta, as a component in a vinaigrette, or as an accompaniment to fish or fowl. Its vibrant flavor brings out the best of whatever you serve it with. Keep pesto frozen in small batches for reviving and remembering summer.

Place the ingredients except the oil in a blender or a food processor, and process until evenly puréed. While machine is running, add the olive oil. If mixture seems too thick, add a little more oil.

RED BERRY SAUCE

═══ YIELD: 2 CUPS ═══

This fresh sauce is best made in summer, but it can also be made with frozen berries. Serve it with fresh fruit, with flan, or to dress up a simple bowl of ice cream. The sauce freezes very well, so double the recipe, and keep it on hand.

Cook cranberries with 1 cup sugar in a 1 quart pot for about 5 minutes. Cool slightly. Cook dissolved sugar and water until it reaches a boil. Turn down heat and simmer for 5 minutes. Wipe the inner perimeter of the pot with a brush dipped in cold water. This will help prevent crystalization of the sugar. Remove from heat and cool for 10 minutes. (This procedure may be done up to this point.) Pour syrup over mixed berries and marinate for at least 30 minutes. Strain the berries from the syrup and combine with the cooked, cooled cranberries. (Reserve and refrigerate strained syrup for other uses.) Place berries in blender or food processor and purée. Strain this purée, taking care to eliminate as many of the fine berry seeds as you can. Flavor with the optional rum or brandy.

2 cups fresh or frozen cranberries

1 cup sugar

1 cup sugar dissolved in 3/4 cup water

2 cups of mixed fresh berries— strawberries, red currants, raspberries

3 tablespoons rum or brandy (optional)

RED WINE SAUCE

YIELD: 2 CUPS

2 tablespoons olive oil or melted butter

2 medium-sized shallots, chopped

1 sprig fresh thyme

1 bay leaf

1/2 teaspoon salt

2 cups red wine —Burgundy, Rhone, or Zinfandel

1 cup beef stock (see "Boiled Beef Dinner" in "Entrees)

juices from deglazing pan in which meat was cooked

1 tablespoon cornstarch dissolved in 2 tablespoons wine (optional)

This basic red wine sauce dresses up lamb or beef. A simple loin lamb chop or lamb roast, when draped with both red wine sauce and roasted onion sauce (see "Sauces") becomes more interesting and certainly more tasty. This sauce freezes very well and you can successfully double it.

Using a 1 quart saucepan, heat olive oil and sauté shallots until they are soft. Add thyme, bay leaf, salt, and red wine. Reduce by half and add beef stock. Reduce again by 1/2. Use some of this liquid to deglaze the pan in which you have sautéed or roasted the meat, scraping up any bits and pieces that are sticking to the pan. Strain the sauce and, if you wish to thicken it, add the cornstarch mixture.

TIP: TO DEGLAZE A PAN SIMPLY MEANS TO POUR IN A QUANTITY OF LIQUID (USUALLY STOCK, SOMETIMES WINE) TO COVER THE BOTTOM OF THE PAN, SCRAPE UP ANY PIECES STICKING TO THE PAN, AND THEN REDUCE THE LIQUID TO INTENSIFY THE FLAVORS.

ROASTED ONION SAUCE

This robust sauce, with its velvety richness and slightly sweet flavor, is usually served with lamb or veal. The onions are slowly roasted in a heavy pot. They are thickened with cooked rice, then puréed along with other aromatics. I have served this as one of a duet of sauces, the other being red wine sauce, and it makes for a really luscious combination (see "Sauces").

Heat oven to 350 degrees. In a 6 cup casserole, toss sliced onion and minced garlic with the melted butter and oil. Cover and roast for 30 minutes, stirring every 10 minutes. Do not let the onions brown. Add the cooked rice and bake for another 10 minutes. Add cream, lemon juice, and salt and pepper. Purée mixture in a food processor. Taste for seasoning and adjust with more lemon juice, salt and pepper, and cream, if necessary. Add the freshly chopped parsley just before serving.

Tip: This makes a tasty soup when thinned with beef or chicken stock. You can change the flavor by using fresh tarragon instead of parsley.

1 **large sweet onion, thinly sliced**

2 **tablespoons melted butter**

2 **tablespoons olive oil**

2 **cloves garlic, minced or pressed**

1 **cup cooked white rice**

1/2 **cup heavy cream**

1 **teaspoon lemon juice**

1/2 **teaspoon salt and freshly ground black pepper to taste**

2 **tablespoons chopped fresh parsley**

ROASTED RED PEPPER SAUCE

═══════ YIELD: APPROXIMATELY 1 1/4 CUPS ═══════

2 large red bell peppers, roasted and skinned

1 clove garlic

1 teaspoon capers

1 tablespoon curry powder

1/2 cup chicken stock or white wine

1/2 cup heavy cream

salt and pepper

This versatile purée is good made with yellow peppers, too. When served cold, it may be mixed with mayonnaise, yogurt, sour cream, or half and half. Just use enough to thin the sauce to a pouring consistency. You can add other flavors, such as chopped fresh herbs or garlic. You can also thin the sauce with stock and/or heavy cream. Serve it either hot or cold.

Roast and skin peppers (see "Basics"). Place roasted peppers and remaining ingredients in food processor. Process briefly and taste for seasoning. Heat gently for use as a warm sauce, since the cream separates easily. This will keep for about a week in the refrigerator.

TIP: YOU CAN ALSO PURCHASE ROASTED RED PEPPERS IN A CAN OR JAR.

TIP: FOR AN EXTRA ZING, ADD 4 ANCHOVIES WITH 1 TEASPOON OF THEIR OIL TO THE PROCESSING MIX.

WHISKEY SAUCE

YIELD: APPROXIMATELY 1 1/2 CUPS

This is a sophisticated accompaniment to bread pudding. It's also great spooned over sliced fresh pineapple. You can substitute brandy, rum or any flavored liqueur for the bourbon.

Cream butter and sugar together in a small bowl. Add egg yolks, beating very well. Place mixture in the top of a double boiler and blend in the cream. Stir constantly until the mixture thickens. It should coat the back of a spoon. Add the bourbon. Pour into a small bowl through a sieve. Serve warm.

8 tablespoons butter, or margarine

3/4 cup confectionery sugar

3 egg yolks

1 cup heavy cream

2 tablespoons bourbon

EMBELLISHMENTS

A few recipes that don't seem to fit into any category, but that add character and depth to a menu, are included in this section. Pickled vegetables, chutney, zucchini relish, and golden turmeric rice are among them, along with fragrant oils infused with herbs. The olive anchovy paste is good piled onto a crackling slice of herbed French bread and the vinaigrette is perfect tossed with roasted or fresh vegetables. I call these embellishments because although they are not necessary to a meal, they do add a certain "zing."

BLUEBERRY CHUTNEY

YIELD: ABOUT 1 1/2 PTS.

2 tablespoons lemon juice

**rind from half a lemon,
cut into thin strips**

1/4 cup granulated sugar

1/4 cup light brown sugar

1 teaspoon ground ginger

1 tablespoon grated fresh ginger

1 teaspoon yellow mustard seed

1/2 teaspoon cinnamon

1 teaspoon curry powder

1/2 teaspoon cayenne pepper

1/2 cup chopped dried apricots

**3 cups fresh blueberries,
rinsed and drained**

Blueberries, blueberries, blueberries! When the market is full of these tender little jewels, and you can't eat another blueberry muffin, blueberry pie, or blueberry pancake, try this chutney. It will keep for 6 to 8 weeks refrigerated, or it can be frozen for months. When you defrost and eat it on a nose-drippingly cold midwinter day, it will instantly transport you to warmth and sunshine. It is particularly good with lamb and chicken and I also like it with an omelet.

Combine all of the ingredients except the blueberries in a 6 cup saucepan and bring to a boil. Cook for 12 to 15 minutes, until mixture begins to thicken. Pick over the blueberries and discard any shriveled or green ones. Stir them into the pot, mix well, and turn off heat. Spoon into clean jars or plastic containers. Refrigerate or freeze.

TIP: BE SURE TO REMOVE ALL OF THE WHITE INNER LINING OF THE LEMON PEEL (THE PITH), WHICH IS QUITE BITTER. IF YOU ARE PLANNING TO FREEZE THE CHUTNEY, YOU CAN SPOON IT INTO HEAVY PLASTIC FREEZER BAGS, PINT OR QUART SIZE. IF YOU ARE STORING IT IN THE REFRIGERATOR, ALLOWING IT TO RIPEN A FEW DAYS BEFORE EATING WILL IMPROVE THE FLAVOR.

CHRISTINE PUDYK'S DILL PICKLES

YIELD: 1 QUART

This is not a pickle to be taken lightly. It is robust and crisp, and its assertive taste stands up to a Boiled Beef Dinner (see "Entrees") or a corned beef sandwich any day. You can slow down its fermentation by storing it in the refrigerator, but I can assure you that it will be eaten before you can say "heartburn." I recommend doubling or tripling the recipe to keep lots on hand. If you prefer to make a large quantity at a time, use any good canning recipe for sterilizing the jars and for sealing and processing the pickles once they are in the jars.

Be sure to sterilize the lid and ring of the jar by heating them to the boiling point in a small pot with water to cover. Pour out the boiling water from the jar and add salt, pickling spice, garlic cloves, and dill. Add the scrubbed cucumbers. Fill jar with cold water and screw on the lid. Store in a cool place for 2 or 3 days.

If you prefer your pickles a little softer, let them sit at room temperature another day or two. Store in refrigerator. Keeps about one month.

TIP: TO SPEED THE FERMENTATION, ADD A WALNUT-SIZED PIECE OF RYE BREAD TO THE PICKLES.

TIP: IF YOU HAVE PLENTY OF STORAGE ROOM IN YOUR REFRIGERATOR, IT IS NOT NECESSARY TO PROCESS THE PICKLES IN A WATER BATH, BUT BE SURE TO BOIL THE JARS AND LIDS, AND TO KEEP THE PICKLES REFRIGERATED ONCE THEY HAVE REACHED THE DEGREE OF FERMENTATION YOU PREFER.

---

1 quart container, thoroughly washed and filled with boiling water

1 tablespoon regular salt

1 tablespoon pickling spice

3 cloves garlic

3 stalks of dill

4 cucumbers (about #3 size), scrubbed, unpeeled

OILS INFUSED WITH HERBS

YIELD: 1 QUART

2 cups fresh herbs of your choice, blanched (see "Basics")

4 cups extra virgin olive oil, divided

So what do you do with fresh basil after you have made tons of pesto sauce? What about that gorgeous plant that you hope will winter over successfully, but never does? Infusing oils with herbs is a great way to extend the aromas and flavors of summer. They can be subtle or strong. Besides their obvious use as part of a salad dressing or mayonnaise, herb-infused oils can take the place of butter or vegetable oil in cooking, or serve as a dip for bread or vegetables. Poured into interesting bottles, they make a great gift to take to a dinner host instead of that ubiquitous bottle of wine. And so easy to make! Blanching the herbs first helps to retain their bright green color and to reduce the possibility of contamination. Strip the leaves from the stalk of the herb and measure the stripped leaves before you blanche them. Blanching will reduce the amount by half.

Blanching will yield about 1 cup of leaves. Purée these with 1 cup of the olive oil. Place this purée in a glass or plastic storage container and add the remaining oil. Cover the container and shake it vigorously. Allow contents to stand for 24 hours. Strain through a triple layer of cheesecloth that has been rinsed in cold water to remove any sizing, or through a coffee filter. (You will have to replace the filter 2 or 3 times.) Store in the refrigerator.

Tip: For a stronger flavor, add seeds of the herb you are puréeing to the infusion. For example, use coriander seed with fresh cilantro, or fennel seeds with fresh fennel, etc. Make a paste of the seeds by first roasting and grinding them and then adding an equal amount of water to the ground seeds before combining them with the fresh herb/olive oil purée. Start with 1 tablespoon of ground seeds (see "Basics") and 1 tablespoon water to see if you like the more pronounced flavor.

OLIVE ANCHOVY PASTE

===== YIELD: APPROXIMATELY 1 CUP =====

Serve this as a condiment to perk up a subtle poached fish, or point up the intense flavors of roasted vegetables. It is very salty, so use it sparingly. Sometimes it is called a "tapenade," especially when capers are added.

In a blender or food processor purée all of the ingredients to a smooth consistency. Store in refrigerator. It will stay fresh for 2 to 3 weeks.

TIP: YOU CAN ADD UP TO 3 TABLESPOONS OF WHITE WINE OR CHICKEN STOCK TO INCREASE THE YIELD OF THIS PASTE, AND TO CUT DOWN A LITTLE ON THE SALT.

5 ounces pitted oil-cured black olives

2 1/4 ounce can flat anchovies, including oil

2 cloves garlic

1 teaspoon Dijon mustard

2 tablespoons olive oil

PICKLED VEGETABLES

YIELD: ABOUT 4 QUARTS

10 cups water

1 cup pickling salt

2 1/2 pounds baby zucchini

1 baby yellow squash

2 1/2 pounds baby carrots

1 pound string beans

4 cups apple cider vinegar

1 1/2 cups water

3/4 cup granulated sugar

2 teaspoons mustard seed

2 teaspoons dried mustard

3 tablespoons pickling spices

8 cloves garlic

2 teaspoons whole black peppercorns

4 dried red peppers

fresh dill or tarragon sprigs

whole fresh wild grape leaves (optional)

When we think of pickles, we usually think of cucumbers or tomatoes, or perhaps string beans. Here is a lovely surprise of baby vegetables, picked at the height of the growing season, perfumed by fresh herbs, and steeped in vinegar. They are a refreshing accompaniment to almost any entrée and present a jewel-like brilliance to a buffet table. If you're like me, you may become seduced by the array of gorgeous produce you see and arrive home with more than you can possibly eat. This is a great solution to the problem.

Combine salt and water in a large bowl and stir until the salt is dissolved. Add the vegetables. Cover the bowl and let stand at room temperature for 24 hours. Drain and rinse the vegetables in several changes of cold water.

Using a large saucepan, bring vinegar, water, sugar, mustard seed, dried mustard, and pickling spices to a boil and simmer for 10 minutes.

Pack the vegetables into hot, sterilized jars and cover them with the hot vinegar/water/ spice mixture. Distribute the garlic, black peppercorns, dried red peppers, and fresh dill or tarragon sprigs evenly. Top each filled jar with a washed grape leaf. Cover the jars with their metal lids and screw tops and process in a boiling water bath for 10 minutes. Cool and store.

Tip: Leave about an inch of the green tops on the baby carrots, but do trim off the stem end of the beans and remove the strings.

Tip: Salting the vegetables first cuts down on spoilage and helps eliminate bacteria.

Tip: Serve these pickled vegetables arranged in bunches around the plate on a bed of fennel or dill fronds.

PLUM CHUTNEY

Chutneys can be smooth, chunky, or both smooth and chunky. They go well with meats and spicy dishes, but also can be eaten with cheese or spread on crackers. Almost any fruit can be "chutnified," but plums are especially luscious. This recipe requires only a little cooking, but it should marinate for at least 12 hours before being served.

Combine all of the ingredients and cook for 10 minutes. Taste and adjust seasonings, if necessary.

1 pound purple plums, pitted and coarsely chopped

1 small red onion, thinly sliced

1/2 cup golden currants

1/3 cup cider vinegar

1/3 cup lemon juice

2 tablespoons brown sugar

2 tablespoons fresh grated ginger

1/4 teaspoon ground nutmeg

1/2 teaspoon roasted ground cumin seed (see "Basics")

RELISHING ZUCCHINI

8 cups grated zucchini or summer squash

4 cups minced onion

2 tablespoon salt

4 cups granulated sugar

2 cups white wine vinegar

2 tablespoon yellow mustard seeds

1 tablespoon fennel seed

5 cloves garlic, minced

2 tablespoons peppercorns

8 pint or 4 quart jars

I have a love/hate relationship with zucchini. I love it steamed, shredded, made into pancakes, in a stir fry, and even breaded and deep fried. I hate it when I have succumbed to Farmers' Market mania and have bought so many different kinds of zucchini or summer squash because it's so beautiful and brilliant and straight or striped and just there, that I am faced with the dilemma of what to do with it when I get home. Here is a recipe that you can make and preserve for winter, when you will once again have a friendly relationship with this vegetable. The beauty of this recipe is that you can mix different kinds of zucchini and it doesn't matter.

Combine the grated zucchini, minced onion, and salt in a large bowl. Chill overnight in refrigerator. Rinse zucchini mixture in cold water and drain well. Blot between layers of paper towels or clean dishcloths. Combine this mixture with the remaining ingredients in a large pot. Bring to a boil over medium heat and simmer for 40 minutes, stirring frequently.

While mixture is cooking, wash jars thoroughly in hot soapy water, then rinse and fill with boiling water to the rim. They should be hot and clean. (Alternatively, you can wash them in a dishwasher through the drying cycle.) When jars are ready and zucchini has finished cooking, taste the mixture and adjust seasoning, if necessary. Empty the jars and pack with mixture to within 1/2 inch of the rim of each jar. Push vegetables down to remove any possible air bubbles, cover jars with lids and screw tops and process in boiling water bath for 15 minutes.

Tip: IF YOU LIKE YOUR RELISH HOT, ADD 1/2 TO 1 JALAPENO PEPPER, RIBS AND SEEDS REMOVED, TO EACH JAR JUST BEFORE PROCESSING.

RENAISSANCE ACRES ORGANIC FARM HERB FRENCH BREAD

=== YIELD: 2 LOAVES ===

Who doesn't love a good loaf of bread? Yes, you can buy very good French bread almost anywhere now, but for a real treat, get yourself a French baguette from Zingerman's or Brewbakers. Herbs from Renaissance Farm are freshly grown and then dried right at the farm. They have an intense flavor that survives the heat of the oven. Forget dinner. Just have bread and cheese and maybe a little wine. Oh, boy.

Heat oven to 350 degrees. Mix all of the herbs with the softened butter and lemon juice. Slice bread to desired thickness and make slanted cuts, 3/4 of the way through the bread, but not all the way through. Spread the herbed butter between each slice and heat through.

TIP: THE HERBED BUTTER CAN BE STORED IN A FREEZER IN AN AIRTIGHT CONTAINER.

TIP: IF YOU ARE A GARLIC LOVER, ADD 3 CLOVES OF MINCED OR SQUEEZED GARLIC TO THE HERBED BUTTER.

8 tablespoons unsalted butter, room temperature

1 teaspoon dried marjoram

1 teaspoon dried rosemary

1 teaspoon dried thyme

1 tablespoon lemon juice

2 tablespoons chopped fresh parsley

2 loaves French bread

TURMERIC RICE

1 tablespoon olive oil

1 clove garlic, minced

1/2 cup minced onions

2 cups long grain rice

3 cups water

1 teaspoon salt

1 teaspoon turmeric powder

3 tablespoons chopped fresh parsley or cilantro

1 teaspoon olive oil or butter (optional)

This is an appetizing and colorful way to serve rice. The lovely yellow-orange turmeric color and the flavor of the sautéed onions accented by chopped parsley or fresh cilantro is a beautiful contrast to almost any entrée. Add a little curry powder or roasted ground cumin to the mixture for a more intense flavor.

Heat olive oil in a 1 quart pot and sauté the garlic and onions until soft. Add rice, stirring to coat grains. Add water, salt, and turmeric. Bring mixture to a rolling boil and stir once or twice. Turn heat down, cover, and simmer for 20 minutes. Remove from burner and let sit for another 15 minutes, covered. Remove cover, add chopped parsley or cilantro, and fluff rice with a fork. Add 1 teaspoon of olive oil or butter, if desired.

VINAIGRETTE MOTHER

I call this a "mother" vinaigrette because with the addition of a few ingredients, its character changes. This is the basic recipe; variations are described in the "Tip" paragraph.

Combine all of the ingredients in a jar with a tight lid and shake vigorously. The result should be emulsified and look a little cloudy. In place of the dried mustard you can use 2 teaspoons Dijon mustard. To vary the flavor, any dried or fresh herbs may be added.

TIP: FOR A MUSTARD VINAIGRETTE, ADD 1 ADDITIONAL TABLESPOON OF DIJON MUSTARD. TO VARY THE FLAVOR, ELIMINATE THE LEMON JUICE, AND SUBSTITUTE ORANGE OR GRAPEFRUIT JUCE AND 1 TEASPOON OF GRATED ORANGE OR GRAPEFRUIT RIND. FOR A TARRAGON VINAIGRETTE, ADD 2 TABLESPOONS OF FRESHLY CHOPPED TARRAGON, AND USE TARRAGON VINEGAR IN PLACE OF THE RED WINE VINEGAR.

1 teaspoon dried mustard powder

1/4 cup olive oil

3 tablespoons red or white wine vinegar

2 teaspoons lemon juice

salt and freshly ground pepper to taste

BASICS

Some techniques and ideas and explanations apply to a
number of the recipes in this book. To avoid repetition, they
are gathered in this section, along with a few others that don't
fit into any other category. You will also find them in the index,
so, with luck, nothing will fall through the cracks.

BLANCHING

Blanching is the process of plunging something, usually a fruit or vegetable, into boiling water, and then in a large quantity of very cold water. This sets the color and flavor and loosens the skins for peeling.

BUTTER

Try to use unsalted butter in cooking, since salted butter retains water, resulting in less fat than is called for in the recipe. To clarify butter, melt any amount in a small container, either on top of the stove or in a microwave. Allow the solids to settle. Carefully spoon or pour off the clear top layer. This is what is called "clarified butter." It does not burn so easily, and is ideal to use when making sauces that call for butter.

CRÈME FRAÎCHE   Yield: 1 cup

Crème fraîche is a thickened cream, somewhat tangy, and its consistency can range from that of sour cream to an almost solid state. It is an ideal addition to sauces because it doesn't curdle when it is boiled. It can be purchased in many supermarkets and specialty stores, but it is also very easy to make. In a glass bowl, add 2 tablespoons of buttermilk to 1 cup of heavy cream and let the mixture sit at room temperature for 8 -24 hours. It will become very thick. It can be spooned over fruit desserts or strudel or berries or anything your heart desires. If you have any left, store it in the refrigerator.

EGGS

All recipes in this book call for large eggs. Whenever possible, take the eggs out of the refrigerator at least an hour before using them. Room temperature eggs seem to produce more volume when they are beaten, especially the whites.

GARLIC

Please use fresh garlic (not garlic powder or pre-chopped garlic or store-bought, peeled garlic), as each recipe indicates. Even though it is convenient, the prepared garlic is not a good substitute for the readily available fresh garlic. When I call for "minced" garlic, you can either mince it with a small sharp knife, or put it through a garlic press.

PEELING CITRUS AND SECTIONING FRUIT

Cut a section from each end of the fruit. Place the fruit on end, and insert the point of the knife between the pith (white inner covering) and the flesh of the fruit. Cutting from top to bottom, and rotating the fruit, remove slices of the peel with the pith attached, until all the peel is removed and no white pith remains on the fruit. Hold the fruit over a bowl and separate segments with a sharp knife, cutting away the knife paper thin membranes between them.

PEELING TOMATOES

To peel tomatoes, prepare a 2 quart pot of boiling water. Have ready a large bowl of cold water. Immerse the tomatoes (don't crowd them; do only a few at a time) in the boiling water for approximately 1 minute. Remove them with a slotted spoon and plunge them immediately into the cold water. Use a sharp knife to remove the skin, which will peel off quite easily using this method, which is called "blanching."

RECONSTITUTING DRIED MUSHROOMS

Place mushrooms in a small saucepan with water to cover. Bring mixture to a boil, reduce heat and simmer for approximately 5 minutes. Turn off heat and cool mushrooms in liquid for 30 minutes or more. Drain through cheesecloth or a coffee filter, reserving the soaking liquid. Rinse mushrooms through several changes of water. It is not necessary to reserve this water. Squeeze mushrooms and remove any tough stems. Wipe the surface of each mushroom to remove any bits of dirt or foreign matter that might remain. Strain the reserved liquid from the first soaking through a fine strainer or a coffee filter once more. If not using liquid in recipe, freeze or store in refrigerator to flavor other dishes.

TO RENDER GOOSE, CHICKEN, OR DUCK FAT

Combine any loose fat and skin from an uncooked goose, chicken, or duck. Combine it, along with 1/2 cup water, in a heavy casserole and cook it on top of the stove until the fat is rendered, or liquified. Be sure to stir it from time to time to keep it from sticking and burning. Strain through cheesecloth or a fine sieve. Keep in refrigerator or freezer until ready to use.

ROASTING PEPPERS

This method works especially well if you have a gas stove and don't mind a bit of clean-up after you are done. Turn gas burner on high and place the whole pepper directly into the flame. The skin will become black and charred. Turn pepper frequently, using long tongs and an oven glove. When the pepper is completely black, remove it from the flame and place it immediately in a paper or plastic bag. Be sure to wait until any sparks that may appear on the pepper (especially the stem) are extinguished. Repeat this step with the remaining peppers. As you become more adept, you may be able to do two or three peppers at a time. The peppers will steam inside the bag, making the skins easier to remove. Leave them to steam for about 10 minutes. Rub off the skins under running water and place the skinned peppers in a colander. Remove stems, ribs, and seeds from each pepper as you remove it from the colander. If you are not using them immediately, store the peppers in the refrigerator in a sealed container.

If you have an electric stove, the best way to char the peppers is under a broiler. Cut them in half, remove seeds and stem, and press down to flatten each half pepper. Trim off ribs with a sharp paring knife and discard them. Place the pepper skin side up on a baking sheet under the broiler. The skins will eventually become charred. Proceed with the recipe by steaming and rubbing off the skins. You can also roast the peppers on an outdoor grill and follow the directions as above.

ROASTING SEEDS

Grinding whole, roasted spice seeds helps to release their essential oils and results in a marvelous aroma and intensified flavor. Spread about 5 tablespoons of seeds in a small sauté pan. Place the pan over medium heat and toast until the seeds are light brown. You should shake the pan from time to time to keep the seeds from burning and to distribute the heat evenly. When seeds have cooled, grind them in a small food processor or a nut grinder. You can also crush them with a mortar and pestle. Store the ground seeds in a tightly covered container.

SWEET TART DOUGH

Here is a sweet tart dough that can be used with some of the pastry based recipes in this book, It makes one bottom of a 9 or 10 inch tart.

1 1/2 cups granulated sugar
1 1/4 cups all purpose flour
1/4 teaspoon salt
1 teaspoon pure vanilla extract
1 egg yolk
1/2 cup cold butter, cut into 8 pieces
1 teaspoon grated lemon rind (optional)

Oops!
Use 1 1/2 TBSP (not cups) of sugar

    Combine sugar, flour, and salt in the bowl of a food processor or mixing bowl. Add butter in small pieces, and process or mix until the mixture is coarse. Add the vanilla and egg yolk and pulse or mix until the dough comes together. This should take only a few seconds. Press dough into a ball and allow to rest for 10 minutes at room temperature, covered with plastic wrap. Roll dough out between 2 sheets of parchment or waxed paper and fit it into a 9 or 10 inch pie pan or tart pan. You may have to push the dough and stretch it to fit into the edges of the pan. Prick bottom and sides of the dough, then proceed with recipe. If proceeding immediately, bake the tart shell at 375 degrees for about 8-10 minutes if you are going to further bake the tart with a filling or for about 12-14 minutes if the tart shell is to be filled without further baking. Wrap and chill or freeze until you need it.

TOASTING NUTS

Heat oven to 375 degrees. To toast nuts, place them on a piece of parchment, waxed paper, or aluminum foil on a baking sheet and roast in oven for 5-8 minutes. Check after 3 minutes, and shake pan to turn nuts over. When the nuts become slightly darker, remove them from the oven. If you have used nuts that still have the skin on them, turn them out onto a clean dish towel, and rub them briskly together. The skins should rub off easily. The nuts will now be ready for use, and their roasty, toasty flavor will enhance any recipe.

VANILLA

A vanilla bean pod is actually the fruit of the celadon orchid. It was first cultivated by the Aztecs, who used it to flavor their chocolate. It is highly aromatic in its processed state. Use only vanilla which is labelled "pure vanilla extract" or "natural vanilla." Imitation vanilla is made entirely of artificial flavorings, mostly based on wood pulp products, and whatever flavor it has is soon dissipated. Strain through a coffee filter once more. If not using liquid in recipe, freeze or store in refrigerator to flavor other dishes.

A FEW MENUS

What to cook? What to save? What to eat? I have assembled these menus to give the reader a helping hand. They range from middle-of-winter potato and leek soup to summer strawberry soup. A tailgate party, an informal buffet, as well as an easy family dinner and brunch also are suggested. All of the recipes appear in this book. I hope they are a springboard to experimentation with other combinations.

MIDDLE OF WINTER

Catherine Reske's Leek and Potato Soup *(p.20)*

Crab Bundles with Roasted Red Pepper Sauce *(p.8, 110)*

Scalloped Tomatoes *(p.73)*

Arugula and Golden Beet Salad with Goat Cheese *(p.18)*

and Mustard Vinaigrette *(p.123)*

Easiest Tart in the World *(p.82)*

EARLY SPRING

Mesclun Salad with Citrus Vinaigrette *(p.24)*

Asparagus with Ginger Sauce *(p.60)*

Roast Lamb with Roasted Onion *(p.48)*

and Red Wine Sauce *(p.108)*

Cauliflower Gratin *(p.65)*

Prickly Pear Sorbet *(p.89)*

Louetta Dieterle's Cinnamon Stars *(p.89)*

SUMMER

Caponata of Zucchini *(p.2)*

and Toasted Sourdough Bread

Tracklements' Smoked Salmon Cakes *(p.55)*

Julienne of Vegetables *(p.66)*

Strawberry Soup *(p.27)*

Grandma's Shortbread *(p.86)*

AUTUMN

Fresh Vegetable Terrine *(p.7)*

Duck Breast with Juniper Port Wine Sauce *(p.36, 105)*

Potato Turnip Purée *(p.71)*

Plum Chutney *(p.119)*

Pears Maxine *(p.91)*

INFORMAL BUFFET

Eggplant "Birds" *(p.37)*

Sliced Cold Harvest Frittata *(p.40)*

Zucchini Relish *(p.120)*

Sliced Tomato/Orange/Onion Salad *(p.28)*

Shrimp and Pork Stuffed Grape Leaves *(p.10)*

Herb Stuffed Pork Loin *(p.41)*

Cauliflower Gratin *(p.65)*

Nemeth's Easy Carrot/Pear Bundt Cake *(p.90)*

A TAILGATE PARTY

Al's Dill Pickle Soup *(p.16)*

Cheddar Cheese Biscuits *(p.3)*

Spinach Pie *(p.51)*

Tracklements' Smoked Salmon Cakes *(p.55)*

Chicken Strudel *(p.35)*

Scalloped Tomatoes *(p.73)*

Peach Pie *(p.87)*

EASY FAMILY DINNER

Mesclun Salad *(p.24)*

Boiled Beef Dinner *(p.34)*

Apple Bread Pudding *(p.79)*

with Custard Sauce *(p.102)*

BRUNCH

Fresh Vegetable Terrine *(p.7)*

Sliced Cold Harvest Frittata *(p.40)*

Fresh Tomato Salsa *(p.63)*

Pasta with Smoked Salmon *(p.45)*

Chocolate Babka *(p.88)*

Citrus Delight *(p.81)*

FARMERS' AND
SHOP OWNERS' LORE

This book honors all the Ann Arbor Farmers' Market and Kerrytown area shop owners, farmers, craftspeople, administrators, bread bakers, fish smokers, etc., who honor the food of the earth. Though these are local people, they surely are representative of similar good people all over the world. (They also represent those market vendors who are not named in this book. We did not have room for all, so we interviewed those who sell food and who had time to participate in this area portrait.) They have contributed their help, knowledge, experience, advice, recipes, and patience to the making of this book, for which we thank them—just as we thank them for bringing us our food.

In his introduction to the first edition of M. F. K. Fisher's *The Art of Eating*, editor Clifton Fadiman wrote, "He minds his belly all the better who is learned in belly lore." Here are the stories of thirty-five farmers and artisan-shop owners.

BENNETT FARMS
JUDI AND DALE BENNETT

"This is the fourth year I've been coming here, twice a week," says Judi Bennett, who drives up from Petersburg, Michigan, near Toledo. "I grew up in the city. We bought our farm in 1975 when we got married. Dale has farmed all his life. We worked in a factory until 1982 [then quit to farm full time]. We tried hogs, but now my husband has 160 acres of corn and [soy]beans he takes to the elevator, and we have fourteen acres of flowers and vegetables. I like the flowers and he likes the vegetables, so it's a tug of war. We have a friend who helps three days a week. We work probably twelve to fourteen hours a day, seven days a week. We have a firewood business in the winter. And we do Christmas wreaths. You try all kinds of things. During the winter I make lists of seeds—what's new, prices, what no one else has . . . I use whatever [seed] catalogs I can get my hands on. You see what works best on your farm. What I like best is pumpkins and gourds and all that fun stuff—the colors, the kids, . . ."

She has to stop talking to wait on a crush of customers, most of whom are buying sweet corn with delicate mixed white and yellow kernels. If a customer asks for a dozen, Bennett bags up thirteen ears. "Do you know how many people of this generation would do this?" asks an older customer who's one of her regulars. The woman from the next stall comes over to help Bennett, who has too many customers at once. "Everyone at the market helps each other," Bennett explains when the crowd thins out. "I think that's how farmers are looked at— honest and generous." ○

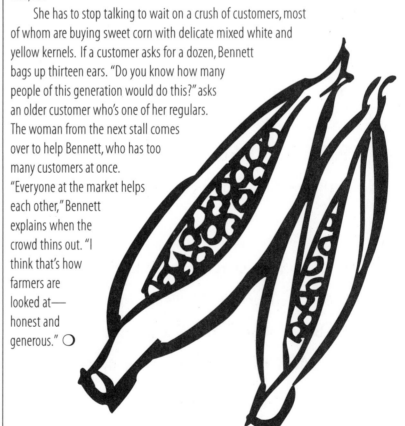

BREWBAKERS
BARRY SEIFER AND SARAH MINOR

It's not unusual to see a shopper leaving Kerrytown greedily munching what looks like a very big bread stick. It may actually be a Provençal Parmesan Breadstick—a skinny fresh loaf infused with herbs, olives, cheese, and roasted garlic—from Brewbakers, which occupies the entire lower level of the Godfrey Building at Kerrytown's northwest corner.

Partners in both marriage and business, Barry Seifer and Sarah Minor opened the combined brewery and bakery in 1997, after almost a year of installing equipment for both processes. Fermentation is the connecting theme. The fermentation of malt, hops, and yeast creates beer; the fermentation of yeast mixed with flour creates bread.

"Brewing and baking are both quite ancient," Seifer says. "They both rely on the management of fermentation. There are ancient Egyptian figures that show baking and brewing together, but we don't know of another [combined] operation around the country. That doesn't mean it doesn't exist, we just couldn't find it. There's no actual cross-over [between the baking and brewing]. The bakery is very low-tech—we have an oven, we have a mixer, and that's it. It's small scale. The brewery is quite high-tech—semiconductors, refrigerator lines, low-voltage sensors. It runs on a larger scale." Bread, at present, is sold only on the premises, but Brewbakers has a distributor who wholesales the beer throughout Washtenaw County.

Seifer has put his management consulting career on hold to become a food artisan, but he briefly returned to the drawing table to design the shop's deep red, gold, and green signage and labels. "I've been involved in the brewing industry as an avocation for about twenty years. I lobbied the [Michigan] legislature for passage of the brewpub bill that involved the right of restaurants to have breweries on site, and I was the original property owner and developer of Grizzly Peak [a popular restaurant and microbrewery that opened in 1994 at the corner of West Washington at Ashley].

"I am a beer lover, but not a brewer. I am our beer designer. Derek Foster is our brewer." Seifer and Minor are Brewbakers' bakers. Seifer went to Montreal's Le Fromentier, which is highly respected for its European artisan approach to bread breaking, "in stints" to learn the baker's art. Le Fromentier helped him plan Brewbakers and furnished its original sourdough starter. ➤

"Sarah and I decided we wanted to have a hearth-bread bakery," he says. Consequently, Brewbakers' interior design melds the old-fashioned look of a brick oven with stunning stainless steel industrial brewing equipment. The high and low are laced together with warm wood counters, railings, and bread carts. All that's visible of the hearth oven is a rounded brick façade decorated with blue, green, and white Italian tiles and punctuated with a small rectangular iron door. But when Seifer opens the door to slide in a bread on a peel (a very long-handled wood paddle just like the ones used in pizza restaurants), he reveals an enormous interior occupied by a stone turntable hearth measuring three feet in diameter. The clever arrangement lets him insert and remove breads quickly. There's also an inconspicuous port into which the baker pours water that humidifies the oven. The attributes of the oven are crucial to the bread's character—the small door inhibits heat loss so the temperature remains more even than in a large-doored oven; the stone and humidity produce a toothsome, but not tough, crust. Seifer and Minor offer the use of this marvelous oven to home cooks who want to bring in their own dough to bake.

Other critical factors are, of course, ingredients and technique. Brewbakers is using organic white and whole wheat flours imported from Canada. As for technique, the shaping of loaves is done on a big wood table, right in view of visitors.

There's a large selection of breads, ranging from white to rye, as well as "fougasse," a bread stuffed with various combinations of cheese, artichoke hearts, olives, and peppers. On Saturdays, the crew also bakes petite pain au chocolat and brioche.

Brewbakers' brewery equipment clambers throughout the big building—even to the outside. The huge tank in the parking lot is a grain silo that holds barley malt, prepared for brewing by a professional maltster. "Like coffee," Seifer says, "the process is a controlled roast that releases different flavor compounds." The silo's screw auger allows delivery of malt into a mill on the third floor. Milled malt is funneled into a scale that's visible above the brewery in the glass elevator well. The scale funnels the stipulated amount of malt down into a copper vessel grist case at the brewery level, where it is "struck" with precisely controlled hot water, forcing the release of enzymes and turning the malt into "wort." Hops are then added, the mix is cooled, then released into the fermentation tank where yeast is added for the final product, which will go into the bottling machine. Brewbakers' magnificent, shiny copper and stainless steel vats look like the dream kitchen for a very industrious giant.

Brewbakers produces six beers, ranging from Hellas German Pale Lager, which, Seifer says, is a simple crisp blend of two malts, to London Porter Ale, which he calls "very complex" with nine malts. The brewery also produces wonderful full-flavored root beer and ginger cream soda.

What's the hardest part of these complex processes? "Repeatability," Seifer says. "It's easy to do. The hard thing is to do it the same every day, despite inevitable variables." ○

PAT DEVULDER

Anthropomorphic, sombrero-topped green peppers dance ecstatically on an 8 by 11 inch sign, one of a series taped along the table edge at Pat Devulder's stall in mid-September. "All Peppers $1.00 per box," it says. Right next to it, another sign featuring a cartoon of a happy looking eggplant with big eyes, arms, and white gloves says, "Little Finger Eggplant, $1.00 per box." The signs are the work of Pat's son, Hector Devulder, who makes them with his computer, using clip-art and lots of exuberant fonts. Flapping in the breeze, they add color and motion to what is already a colorful and active booth.

Besides making the mirthful signs, Hector helps Pat with the heavy work of loading the truck with vegetables and flowers on Tuesday and Friday nights and unloading it at the market on Wednesday and Saturday mornings. Weekdays he leaves for his job at a printing company. Pat's daughter, Linda Rose, replaces her brother at the stall at about 8:30 a.m. after seeing her son, Vincent, off to school. Pat's husband, Ralph, who is a full-time farm manager at a larger farm, does the family farm's seeding, planting, spraying, and tractor work. They're as youthful and muscular a bunch as the energetic vegetables on Hector's signs.

The soil on their farm, Pat says, is part "mucky loam," which contains a lot of organic matter and so is good for spinach, radishes, and beets, and partly "sandy loam," which is good for tomatoes, peppers, and flowers. Lots of customers make a beeline for Devulder's booth to buy plastic bags of spinach because they know it's well washed. "We wash it in a big tank," she says. "We push it down to soak it good. Then we put it in big black tubs in the cooler to let it drain. It's good raw in salad or cooked."

Pat grows the usuals, including rhubarb, beets, broccoli, scallions, and radishes. ("Radish sandwiches are good," she claims.) She also has a big selection of fresh herbs. Cilantro and parsley, she says, are the big sellers. Although she thinks of growing flowers as a hobby, they actually take up half her market space. Like the Devulders themselves, there is something especially hearty about the zinnias, black-eyed Susans, sunflowers, snapdragons, mums, and other cut flowers and flowering potted plants ready for home gardeners. ○

TIPS

Radishes make great munchies simply dipped in a bowl of softened butter and then a bowl of salt, according to Pat Devulder.

To dry herbs, tie them in bunches and hang them upside down in a dark cool spot (farmers use their barn rafters). Pat Devulder thinks that herbs dried in this way are more flavorful than those dried in electric dehydrators.

Cookbook co-author Ricky Agranoff has devised a "mini-hothouse" (actually a "cold-house") method of keeping fresh herbs. Place the herbs upright in a container half-filled with water, so that the stems, but not the tops, are submerged. Then place the container in a plastic bag. Tie the bag shut over the tops of the herbs. Punch one or two holes in the bag for air circulation. Keep refrigerated. Change water frequently.

BOB AND LOUETTA DIETERLE

Viewed from above, the Ann Arbor Farmers' Market would look like an upper-case letter E, with its long spine slightly extended in both directions. The E has two hot spots. One, the market office, is situated on the top crossbar of the E. The other is the vibrant corner at the bottom left of the E shape. Bob and Louetta Dieterle occupy the market's place of honor at the inside elbow of that corner. The view from there lets them observe the busy comings and goings of the entire market, and Bob Dieterle is the market's most experienced observer. He has been a market vendor longer than anyone else. He first came to help and play at his parents' stall in 1924, when he was five years old.

Back then, the market was still at the corner of Main and Ann, and Bob vaguely remembers that the line for a stall was so long that it extended along the entire block to the armory at Fifth and Ann. Until twenty years ago, he says, he'd "never missed a Saturday, year 'round." Now, the Dieterles skip the winter Saturdays.

Bob's parents, Chris and Vera Dieterle, bought the family farm in 1917, shortly after they married. It's a bumpy half-mile ride west along a dirt road off Saline-Milan Road south of Saline. Bob remembers snowy winters and muddy springs when he'd hitch a team of horses to his mother's 1934 Ford V-8 and pull it out to the main road so she could go to market. At the end of the afternoon, he'd go out to wait for her so he and the horses could pull the car back. On market days, the family removed the V-8's front seat and filled it with vegetables and meats.

Bob and Louetta were married on his twenty-first birthday, February 1, 1941. They shared home and farm with Bob's parents for the next fifteen years, eventually becoming the senior generation and parents of two children. Now age has slowed them down a bit, and Bob has undergone some patching, including replacement of both knees and both hips. In their younger days, they grew hay, soybeans, and corn on ninety-five acres. They raised hogs, cows, and chickens, and they churned their own butter and cottage cheese. They even used to bring dressed muskrats and raccoons to market, though Bob says, "Never ate one in my life."

"I used to bring little bunnies for Easter," Bob says, "but you can't do it now." For a time in the 1980's they kept donkeys, sheep, and goats to provide 125 pints of blood serum to a lab every week. Bob was fond of the animals and tells stories about them, including one about the time he took some donkeys to a nearby school for a demonstration. For a long time after, one of them kept trying to go back.

Louetta is down to 300 dahlia plants from a high of 600. Each plant has to be hand-staked and tied when it's in flower, then dug up each fall and replanted each spring. She used to pull all-nighters, cutting dahlias on moonless nights with a flashlight clasped under one arm. Her dahlias are so impressive that a Detroit florist used to come to buy them all, but the Dieterles, not wanting to disappoint their local customers, finally worked out a plan:

Louetta returned with a second load of flowers after the Detroiter had purchased all of the first.

Now the Dieterles rent out most of their land but keep a half-acre garden from which they harvest a lot of vegetables, berries, and a supply of magnificent flowers—daisies, peonies, snapdragons (which Louetta calls, simply, "snaps"), delphiniums, and, especially, the dahlias.

Puffballs (big round mushroom-like fungi) grow on their property, and if conditions have been warm and rainy enough, they'll bring a few to market each week in October. Longtime customers know to ask for them; they're suitable for all mushroom recipes and can make a main dish on their own simply breaded and sautéed.

The Dieterles are worried about the economic future of small-scale truck farming. "If you had to pay the price to make ends meet, you wouldn't think it's so wonderful," Louetta says. With age catching up with them, they're not sure how much longer they'll stay around. "Every year, I say it's the last," Bob says. But problems or not, the Dieterles of the Farmers' Market embody the essence of the productive and caring life. ○

DUKE AND LINDA DONAHEE

FARM RECIPE

Donahee likes lima beans boiled down with loose pork sausage for about half an hour. Another Donahee favorite consists of lima beans simmered for about 45 minutes with dried apricots or other dried fruits.

TIPS

Donahee says you can tell a ripe cantaloupe by its netting. Yellow skin below the netting indicates a ripe melon. Heavy netting, he says, indicates a sweet one.

Donahee says Brussels sprouts picked after a frost seem sweeter. "Boil 'em, drain 'em, put on butter, salt, and pepper. That's good enough for me!" he says.

"Duke" (Lawrence) Donahee's experience proves that the market is not only for the customers, but also by the customers. In addition to an Ann Arbor Farmers' Market booth, the Donahee family operates a stand at their farm north of Ann Arbor. Farm stand customers, Donahee says, want their zucchinis to be real big, so they'll get their money's worth, and their lettuce to be traditional American iceberg, which is a good vehicle for bottled dressings. Farmers' Market customers, on the other hand, he reports, want their zucchinis to be tiny so they'll be less seedy and more colorful on the plate, and they pass by iceberg lettuce, demanding the more flavorful (and more trendy) leafy varieties.

Adjusting their output for two different sets of customers is just one of the seemingly endless number of things this vibrant family performs. They also work two different sets of jobs! Duke, like his father (Lewis—also called "Duke") before him, farms from eight o'clock in the morning until one in the afternoon, and then he goes to work as a furnace operator, heat-treating and hardening steel gears for Ford Motor Company until ten at night!

Linda farms when she's not putting in her eight hours as a claims processing rep at St. Joe's hospital. Duke's elder son (called, of course, "Duke") is also doing the Ford Motor/farming combo. His younger son, Steven, works on the farm and helps at the market. All this hard work "couldn't kill you," Duke says. "My dad worked until he was eighty-four years old—subdivision retirees don't live so long."

Farming, being a seasonal occupation, still leaves some extra time, so the Donahee clan also splits and sells firewood, runs a snow-removal business, and retails and wholesales 5,000 flats of bedding plants from three greenhouses.

The Donahees' market tables are always heavily laden with big, round, muscular looking produce, including bulbous, violet-striated Lebanese eggplants. "How I got growing them," Duke says, "is that the seed company got mixed up and put the seed in with my order. I decided to plant it anyway, and the customers liked them." ◯

FROG HOLLER
KEN KING

Oh, there's none so rare

As can compare

With King Cole and

his fiddlers three.

What do broccoli, cauliflower, kohlrabi, kale, collard, and cabbage have in common? The "cole," "caul," or "ca" sound that marks them all as members of the "cole" (hence "cole slaw") family. (The dictionary gives "cole" as a derivation of the Greek and Latin for "stalk.") Ken King, who with his wife, Cathy, owns Frog Holler Farm, is full of that sort of loving information about plants, planting, and nutrition. Although he is a lean man, rather than the fat old soul who usually accompanies the nursery rhyme, King nevertheless is a sort of ecologically sound version of his more sybaritic predecessor. According to The Annotated Mother Goose, by William S. Baring-Gould and Ceil Baring-Gould, there is a large earthwork, perhaps the remains of a Roman theater, in Colchester, England, which is popularly known as "King Cole's kitchen." Ken King, who loves to cook, started out as a restaurateur, and he and his three sons are fiddlers.

Some of the concerns of the 1960's hippie movement have become mainstream health and environmental issues of the 1990's, kept alive in the interval by idealists like the Kings. In 1970, Ken and two partners opened Indian Summer Natural Foods, a vegetarian restaurant, on State Street near the University of Michigan campus. At that time, organic produce was not easily available, and the young restaurateurs decided it would be best to grow their own. That became possible in 1972 when Ken and Cathy King were able to buy Frog Holler Farm near Brooklyn, Michigan.

Because she wanted, in her old age, to see her wildlife sanctuary and farm go to someone who would love and preserve it, conservationist Cora Lees Gesell (a friend of Rachel Carson's), sold it to the Kings at a below-value price they could afford. Located in the rolling Irish Hills about thirty miles southwest of Ann Arbor, it's beautiful land with maple and ash groves and with a ten-acre lake in the middle, King says. Eventually, the restaurant's three partners split up, remaining friends, and the Kings took up farming full time. (To the confusion of some customers, one of King's restaurant partners, Rick Peshkin, now runs a wholesale and retail business that grew out of his relationship with Frog Holler Farm and still bears its name.) ➤

King is casual, rather than dogmatic, about organic farming. "We don't try to proselytize," he says. "More than half our people [customers] are not directly concerned. They just want the quality." He can cite studies showing that proteins synthesized by plants grown chemically appear to be more brittle than those of plants grown organically. Recently, he says, a scientist has compared computer images of plant cells. The organically grown material, King says, "looks like tie-dyed T-shirts—they're beautiful and have a symmetry. The chemically grown ones have broken shapes." He withholds judgment, saying, "It's nothing I can confirm." But he does use only organic methods of farming and he does know he runs a successful farm with good yield and healthy plants without using chemical fertilizer or insecticides.

Chemicals are needed, he says, only on big farms, where heavy machinery breaks down the protective skin of topsoil, where the land has been overused, or where neglect has broken the cycle of natural fertilization with its resulting healthy plants able to withstand bugs and diseases. "Compost," he says, "is pretty well balanced. It feeds the plants at the right rate, without juggling things [chemical applications] all the time. It's time-consuming, and we never make much money, which is okay. Sometimes it seems like there's a little imbalance, like when a customer says 'O-o-o-h, a dollar and a quarter is a lot for that,' but not many do that."

King's mesclun, or mixed salad greens, for example, runs about $10 a pound; but a pound is enough to feed eight to ten people, and the work that goes into the pound dictates the price. Frog Holler mesclun is a changing combination of baby red and green lettuce, radicchio, arugula, parsley, chives, bronze fennel, sorrel, red chard, and edible flowers like nasturtiums and violas, or johnny-jump-ups. The Kings manage to grow lettuce even in hot weather by using an area of wet black ground. "It's hard to get into it," King says, "because [the soil is so rich that] the weeds grow real tall there, and it's hard to break up." In the fall, they grow lettuce on higher ground, where the drainage is better and the air is a little warmer, providing some frost protection.

In July, when we spoke with him, King was selling huge collard greens—a typical leaf measures about 8 inches by 10 inches. "Collards are the most primitive cole," he explains, "flat and primitive." All coles are rich in essential calcium and minerals. King tells a story of a Scottish doctor who was said to have traveled the countryside looking for a place where no coles were grown. Finding one, he nailed up his shingle, knowing that the area residents were sure to have more than the average numbers of illnesses.

Dickens, he says, wrote in one of his stories about using collard greens tied up as a bag in which to cook fish. With the stem removed and the leaf blanched to soften it, a collard leaf can be used as a wrap for cooking in the same way that cabbage leaves are used. A regular customer stopped by while we were there. She was going to stir-fry collards with bean sprouts and "lots of garlic" and serve the mixture over brown rice for a macrobiotic meal.

"We try to do everything nice," King says. He is grateful to his customers and they to him, so the end of transactions, he says, often are 'Thank you,' and 'Thank you back.'"○

GARDEN WORKS
ROB MACKERCHER

Rob MacKercher of Garden Works doesn't have to drive very far to get to the Ann Arbor Farmers' Market. His four-acre farm nestles just outside the city limits. Its modest entry branches off Pontiac Trail just south of M-14. Although the highway is nearby, the farm is serenely quiet, and MacKercher is a quiet man. He is one of the young growers who have consciously entered farming with idealistic intentions of taking care of the ecosystem.

Although not from a farming family, MacKercher grew up in the farming community of Canton. "It [farming] was all around," he says. "I befriended someone in high school who had an organic farm and I worked there summers." He also became interested in the writings of Wendell Berry, especially Berry's book *The Unsettling of America*, a philosophical and inspiring examination of the history and future of farming in the U.S. MacKercher also is a member of the highly respected Food First, a national organization that publishes information concerning the interrelationships of economics, community, and agriculture.

MacKercher first came to Garden Works in 1989, when a friend of his was managing it, but it was on the verge of closing. He eventually leased the farm from its owner, taking on the basic responsibility of running it in harmony with the like-minded people who work with him. He usually has three to seven co-workers in the summer and two or three in the winter.

The little farm is neatly divided into plots for spring—spinach and other salad greens which, by sequential plantings, he keeps going until August; summer—spinach, kale, collard greens, broccoli, herbs, etc.; and fall—pumpkins and potatoes. There's a greenhouse for starting summer seedlings and for raising winter and year-round crops. MacKercher is one of the area's few suppliers of wheatgrass. High in vitamins and minerals, it can be chewed, but, more usually, it is used for juice by health enthusiasts. The majority of Garden Works' wheatgrass crop goes to places such as Joe-Joe's Cafe and Raw Juices. (Joe-Joe's, on North Fourth half a block south of the Farmers' Market and next door to the People's Food Co-op, is the market area's answer to a greasy spoon, serving delicious nutritious home-style cooking and healthy juices.) Garden Works also uses the greenhouse all year to raise flats of sunflower sprouts. These sprouts have a wonderful, meaty character and high nutritive value.

The farm's big barn is filled with dusky grey light and inhabited by a similarly colored cat. It dates only to 1970, and its upper story had to be replaced after a tornado ripped it off in 1989. Nevertheless, it has a timeless, Tolkien-ish character, partly because of its woodsy aroma and partly because high, wooden garlic racks create a mysterious, half-lit maze. Garden Works produces over 2,000 pounds of garlic each year. Garlic is planted in October and harvested in July. MacKercher uses the barn to store the sorted bulbs in the wooden racks. Bulbs grown from cloves saved from the previous year's crop are larger than those started from the tiny cloves that ripen in the seed pods at the top of the garlic stalk.

MacKercher has not been coming to market long enough to have a permanent booth, and his quiet mien makes whatever temporary stall he's at somewhat inconspicuous. Regulars, though, search it out for the extremely robust quality of his produce. Take the spinach, for example.

"A lot of people like our spinach," he says. "It's organic. We do irrigate it a lot. There's not one magic thing—it's everything we do. People question why it's more expensive. Everything is from seed, not plugs. All cultivation is by hand. We don't use any herbicides and we don't use heavy machinery, which would compact the soil. We harvest it and sell it within a day—California produce at the grocery store can be four or five days old. We rinse it, but any produce you buy, you should still rinse it. I like spinach with whole grain rice, maybe with a little wild rice, or you can add lentils if you want more protein. You can cook them [rice and lentils] separately or together. When the rice is almost done, you can add some carrot shavings. You can steam the spinach in a little olive oil, covered, for a few minutes with a little salt (I only use sea salt), maybe add toasted sesame seeds. You can substitute kale or collard greens for the spinach."

In the fall, he's likely to do a similar recipe using squash instead of rice. He grows, among others, a variety of squash called delicata; it's an oblong, yellow-and-green-striped squash that, he says, "is very sweet and tender. You cut it in half, scoop out the seeds, bake it face [cut side] down in a little water. After it's steamed thoroughly, you flip it up and bake some more—that candies up the squash."

Garden Works produce is also available at the People's Food Co-op, Arbor Farms, Whole Foods, the Cass Corridor Food Co-op in Detroit, and at several area restaurants. ○

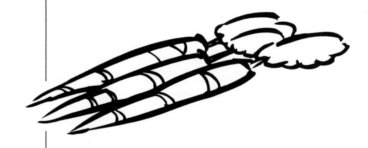

DELORES GRACIA

Curly-haired Delores Gracia brings both plants and family to the market. Her parents, Louis and Bessie Vena, were farmers whose names and vocation echo down the generations. At first, it seemed as if Delores would be the only one of Louis and Bessie's children to remain in farming. But over the years, several of her brothers and sisters returned to the land—and to the market, where they are now a good-humored network that contributes to the market's familial atmosphere.

Delores's sister Tina Koski has the adjacent market stall; sister-in-law Carol Vena, wife of Delores's brother Louis, shares a stall with their daughter, Denise Block; niece Devena Rohn has a stall across the big aisle; and son Mario Gracia has a stall at the Royal Oak farmers' market. Delores is now helped by her daughter, Bessie Newbery. Among other things, they sell cherry tomatoes from the row that the family considers the property of Bessie's children: future farmers Joey, four, and Brandy, two.

Unlike growers who doubt that future generations will be able to earn a living in small-scale farming, Delores believes that Joey and Brandy will be able, because part of the family's income comes from the Gracia Greenhouses. Her parents constructed their first greenhouse when Delores was twenty-one. In January, she begins preparing containers and planting flower and vegetable seeds there. Some of the resulting seedlings will be sold at wholesale and some at the market as starter plants for home gardeners (the greenhouse is open for retail sales during planting season); all the rest will be planted in the fields to grow the produce the family sells at market.

We were chatting with Delores Gracia in early September when a man stopped to buy green peppers that he intended to cut up and freeze for a winter supply. He asked for fifteen. Gracia threw in a sixteenth free. She, too, freezes the green peppers, simply removing the white inside ribs, dicing the rest, and freezing them in plastic bags for use in winter cooking. Before freezing red peppers, she roasts them in the oven until their skins can easily be slipped off, then lays them flat in plastic bags. She also grows Italian sweet peppers, which customers use either raw in salads or cooked in stir-fries. And she has slim Anaheim medium hots, which she recommends used cut up in salsa or baked whole, stuffed with a mixture of ground beef, cooked rice, and onion.

Spring starter plants include a huge range of garden herbs. Five years ago, the Gracia family began assembling kitchen-window herb pots. An oval pot with rosemary, sage, parsley, oregano, basil, and thyme plants, for example, is an indoor mini-garden. During winters, Gracia makes grave blankets and wreaths to sell at market. There's a little time off, then it's back to the greenhouse and the cycle of growth she loves.

"Sometimes I'll go out in the evening," Gracia says, "and someone will ask, 'Where are you going?' And I'll tell them, 'To see my babies,' the plants." ○

VIRGINIA HAMMOND

"You know I wrote a cookbook, too," Virginia Hammond told us when we stopped for a chat at her stall one sunny September morning. She rummaged around in the back of her truck and pulled out a few copies of *Home on the Range—Saving Grandma's Secrets*. Hammond wrote the cookbook in 1989 at the urging of her friends and as a fund-raiser for Faith Lutheran Church in Saline. Her photo in the front of the book doesn't, at a quick glance, look much like the very contemporary Hammond, who is blond and vigorous. "I told the photographer, 'I want you to make me look like I'm one hundred,'" she said. He dressed her up to look like a nineteenth-century grandmother in a lacey white bonnet tied under her chin with a black velvet ribbon. She wore a big-collared old-fashioned dress, and by coincidence (play-acting goes only so far) she was puffy-faced from a case of poison ivy. The reason she did it was to honor the people who taught her to cook, especially her mother-in-law, Minnie Hammond.

She thumbed through the pages with us, pausing to remark fondly about various recipes. "Have you ever made pretzels?" she asked. (We hadn't.) "That's a good recipe; this is the best recipe for molasses cookies, and you want to try this orange slice cake, too." The pretzel recipes require ingredients that probably have never even been seen by most city-dwelling market customers. Pretzels get their shiny surface from being dipped in a lye and soda solution just before baking. Consequently, the recipe advises greasing the cookie sheet with beeswax. (In a nod to modern times, it says nonstick cookie sheets can be used, though not aluminum.) Pretzel stands are appearing at shopping malls; maybe lye and beeswax will return to home kitchens, too. Another old-time country recipe begins, "Dress a young pig about six-weeks-old, and thoroughly wash it inside and out . . ." After cleaning and stuffing, the "youngster," as Hammond calls the pig, is placed in the baking pan in a kneeling position. If served at Christmas time, it can be garnished with an apple in the mouth and holly around the neck. Why are people not doing this much anymore? Suckling pigs may be ready for revival, too; they're available, on order, from Sparrow Meat Market in Kerrytown.

Most of Hammond's recipes, like scalloped corn, Grandma's baked beans, and peanut butter fudge, are easy and call for readily available ingredients. In addition to being practical and appealing, they also contain lots of general cooking information. For example, it's uncommon to make ice cream cones at home because few people own the cone-shaped iron needed to form them, but Hammond's recipe suggests baking the dough in a waffle iron to make ice cream sandwich covers. "Any stiff batter, such as brownies, can readily be cooked in a waffle iron," she said.

Virginia Hammond has been coming to the Ann Arbor Farmers' Market since 1952. She wonders how much longer local farms will survive. Housing developers are offering high prices for farmland, and she frequently gets inquiries about her 280 acres. "They'd grab it so quick if we let them," she says defiantly. In the meantime, her stall tables are covered with red-and-white checked tablecloths and heaped with whatever is in season—leeks, peppers, salad greens, spinach, tomatoes, etc. She is an organic farmer by default—she follows her family's old-fashioned methods of using natural compost and avoiding chemical insect sprays. Last year she noticed melon leaves were being eaten by bugs. She defeated them by sprinkling the plants with her own compound of garlic and hot pepper powders.

"This market is unique. It's the best in the United States," she says. "Well, I haven't been to all of them. Other markets are commercial; they [the vendors] buy every darn thing—here you grow it yourself. I don't know what makes it so unique. The people, I think. I don't make that much money," she says, "but I feel the people need good food." ○

HILL O'BEANS
SMILING CAT TEA MERCHANTS
MIKE AND ROXANNE POTTER

"There are two-hundred and eighty-six things in a grape that can affect taste," Mike Potter says. "There's almost double that in coffee."

"A lot of times people ask me about coffee, so I talk and talk, and they leave, and after a while I notice that they're gone," confesses Mike Potter.

In the early 1990's, Mike and his wife, Roxanne, decided they'd like to have a business of their own. Mike was working as a gemologist at the time; Roxanne was working, as she still does, as an admitting person in the emergency room of a Livonia hospital. While traveling, the couple encountered a little food shop that specialized in coffee; because they loved coffee, they decided "that was it." They took up a serious study of coffee and tea.

When, in 1994, they felt they'd learned enough and had found suppliers, they opened Hill O'Beans. They moved it to Kerrytown in 1995, and as tea sales grew, expanded its name to Hill O'Beans/Smiling Cat Tea Merchants. The "smiling cat" is their own big, black "rather stand-offish" cat Pixl, who one day jumped up on the table ("a no-no," Mike says) and stuck his nose into a cup of hot tea. The Potters thought the funny face he made looked like a smile, and then, Mike says, "I thought a lot of people who like tea like cats."

SMILING CAT TEA MERCHANTS

As he admits, Mike likes to talk about coffee. "We sell specialty coffees," he says. "They are class one, which means they are allowed only up to five minor defects in 300 grams of beans." A big poster on the shop's wall features photos of coffee beans making it "easy to see the difference between the graded classes. "Beans are judged for characteristics like uniformity of size, specific gravity, ripeness, and taste.

"Coffee is the second-largest cash commodity in the world, after oil. There are fifty-seven coffee-producing countries. Because coffee is in demand, farmers can sell their crop even if they don't spend the extra time and money to ensure top quality.

"Quality begins with the seed, then goes on to the care the farmer takes in growing the seedling. It has to be carefully trimmed so it will turn into a bush that bears good fruit. Fruit has to be hand-picked, since there is ripe and unripe fruit on the same branch. Unripe beans make bitter coffee—it's like eating a green apple. Ripe cherries [as the beans are called] are red; unripe are green. The bean contains two seeds back-to-back, like the halves of a walnut; if there's only one seed, it's called a 'peaberry.'

"The next step is getting that seed out. There are a number of ways, and each of them has a number of right and wrong approaches. For example, they can soak the cherries, but then stale water gets into the beans; or the cherries can be dried by literally forcing them in a clothes drier. Or, correctly, they can be slowly and carefully dried in the sun—and then there can't be rain.

"I was at a seminar, and a Guatemalan coffee grower was there, and he said they dry their beans in the sun for eleven days. Someone asked, 'Do you have a weather forecaster?' And he said, 'Yes.' And they asked, 'A meteorologist?' And he said, 'No, a witch doctor.'

"Storage [before roasting] can make a difference too. It's a small point, but the bean is still in a membrane sac, or parchment. Without that, it can dry out. In milling, the parchment is removed. The coffee is sorted after that. Different coffees have to be roasted differently. Beans grown at four thousand feet are heavier and denser than beans grown at three thousand feet. If they're roasted together, well, it's like baking a muffin and a croissant at one time in the same oven at the same temperature—one will be burnt, the other underdone.

"We bought a roaster when we started the store, but roasting takes a renaissance person. We were exposed to people with years of experience and they started sending us samples, and we thought, 'Oh, wow.' Roasting brings out different flavors. All coffee has a bitter substance that evaporates at four hundred and eleven degrees. Now we're buying from the finest micro-roasters in the country. We call them; they roast it and ship it; and I get it in forty-eight hours. I buy enough for a week."

Tea has risen to 40 percent of sales at the shop. Mike is a tea drinker, as enthusiastic in his conversations about tea as in those about coffee. He carries loose and bagged teas from around the world.

"It's a very similar situation [to that of coffee]," Mike says. "You're rehydrating the leaves and releasing oils, gasses, and acids."

Smiling Cat Tea Merchants sells by mail order as well as through the store. Their e-mail address is scteamerch@earthlink.net; the out-of-town phone number is 800-440-TEAS. ○

Hill O'Beans
...not just coffee...

JAY JARVIS

We met Jay Jarvis and his kids — thirteen-year-old Jennifer, nine-year-old Amber, and eight-year-old Eric— in mid-August. It was their first day as vendors at the market. The family is new to farming. "I'm doing it for my kids," Jay said, "so they don't have to work for nobody else. We'd been living in a trailer park for fifteen years, and we wanted to buy a farm. We applied for a farm home loan [and were disappointed when nothing much happened]. But the week after my mom died, I got a letter that they were ready to process my loan. I thought, 'Wow. Mom is watching out for us.' I'd been working at a horticultural supply company, and I met people who know farming and learned from them. It's hard but gratifying work. We had a roadside stand till now and were kind of renting land then. Now I bought twenty acres and can [grow enough to] come here. We're waiting to get a [permanent] booth."

The Jarvis kids not only know how to grow and sell vegetables; they also cook. "My dad was a cook on a boat on the Straits of Mackinac," Jay said. "The kids all started cooking when they were about five years old. Jennifer was about seven when she cooked her own dinner right from scratch. They know how to make macaroni the old way, right from scratch. One day my wife's niece came over and [seeing the macaroni and cheese] asked, 'Where's the box?'"

While we talked to Jay, the kids tended the stall. "We'll take care of it, Dad," Jennifer said. We asked her if scallions grew the same way as fresh young onions. "No," she said. "Scallions make flowers and reseed themselves. The onions multiply and we divide them and replant the small ones. Scallions are more for salads. Spanish onions have more zing and are good for potatoes or pasta." Their table also held potatoes (Amber thought the different varieties tasted a little different from each other); peppers, including a Ram's Horn variety for its shape, which Amber recommended for salad or pizza; cucumbers; and other summer fare. ○

KAPNIK ORCHARDS
JANICE KAPNICK AND
SHARON SHAFFER

In mid-1997, after thirty-nine years at the Farmers' Market, it seemed likely that Janice Kapnick would be cutting back sometime in the next few years. In early winter, that's just what happened: she sold part of her land to developers and turned over management and ownership of Kapnick Orchards' remaining sixty acres to her daughter, Sharon Shaffer. Kapnick and orchard manager Scott Robertello will continue to do the Farmers' Market stall while Shaffer runs the orchard's retail shop.

Janice married Charles Kapnick in 1958. They both had agricultural backgrounds. "My dad was a gentleman farmer," she says, "and I had the championship Angus steer at the 1949 state 4-H show. Charles's parents were truck farmers in Deerfield, Michigan, and he earned a horticultural degree at Michigan State." The young couple bought eighty-eight acres of farmland when they married and eventually expanded to 140 acres.

Their farm had fruit trees, and they added more—apple, peach, plum, sweet cherry, nectarine, and pear. They also planted raspberries and blueberries. The sandy soil in their area on the ancient shoreline of Lake Erie, Kapnick says, is well suited to growing fruit. They also grew vegetables to bring to market and to sell at their own year-round market at Kapnick Orchards near Tecumseh. They reared three daughters and had a good life, she says. But since Charles died in 1995, it's been hard, not only for Janice, of course, but also for the orchard, since he was the expert. "Growing good fruit," she says, "takes a person knowledgeable of good tree pruning and spraying."

Her beaming face is familiar to most market regulars. She no longer brings vegetables to market. Fruit, she says, is less time-consuming to grow and harvest. The Kapnick Orchards stall is also well known for the big assortment of baked goods baked by Shaffer, whose offerings include pies, coffee cakes, and twenty kinds of bread, the most popular being a pecan-cinnamon loaf and apple fritter bread.

"I couldn't tell you how many trees we have," Kapnick says. "We have about two thousand young trees. We have about twenty varieties of apples—I'd have to think it out. None of our original trees are left. When they're not paying their way, you take them out and plant new ones. First we sow [an empty patch] with sorghum and cover crops, then we plow it under to nourish the ground. We rotate where we plant the trees. A peach tree lasts about twelve to fifteen years. We do have some apple trees that are thirty-eight years old—they're getting to where they should be replaced. We have different varieties of apples and peaches to make a long season. [For example] Flaming Fury peaches. I have a friend who cross-breeds them; they run from early to late season. Peaches that ripen mid- to late season come off the stone easier, so they're better for canning and freezing. During peach season, I'm so busy we just eat ours fresh. Otherwise I like to bake peach cobbler and fresh peach pie. Apples—Vista Bella is for summer eating; they're only good for a week or two, you can't store them, and they get mushy fast. Early Transparent is good for applesauce and pies; they ripen in July and are thin-skinned and sour. Late apples like Mutsu, Fuji, and Braeburn store well.

"We also ship apple gift boxes and other fruit boxes all over the U.S.A., from November first to January fifteenth. Customers just give us their list of addresses and we do the rest. We also make over one thousand fruit baskets at Christmas time and throughout the year, filled with many fruits, candies, nuts, jams, or whatever the customer wants." ○

ESTHER KAPP

"A lot of people ask us if the corn was picked this morning," snorts Esther Kapp, as she unloads her truck at six o'clock on an October Saturday morning. It's still dark. "We leave home at four-thirty in the morning. The corn was picked the night before. We don't have floodlights like a football field. But many nights we're out packing tomatoes until one o'clock," she says.

The vegetables are still nose-tickling fresh. Pre-dawn is the market's magic moment. The growers' camaraderie adds excitement and good will. As pink clouds fill the sky, the multitude of sparrows nesting in the ivy on the side of the adjacent Kerrytown Marketplace begin chirping self-importantly.

"The birds were so noisy one morning, we had to scream at each other," says Kapp, whose stall is only a few yards from the ivy. "It sounds like they're all happy." Unloading is interrupted by a small number of customers who make it their habit to come early and are consequently well known to the growers.

The market is a second home to Kapp. Her parents, Francis and Lucile Maulbetsch, helped to start the original Farmers' Market, located on the grounds of the old Ann Arbor Courthouse. Winters, the market moved into lumber sheds that stood where the Kerrytown parking lot is now. Kapp attended Jones School (now Community High) across the street from the market and then went on to Ann Arbor High (now the UM Frieze Building), graduating in 1953. When she and Richard Kapp married, they bought a farm not far from the Maulbetsch farm on North Territorial Road north of Ann Arbor. "If they needed extra help, we were there, and if we needed extra help, they were there," Kapp recalls fondly. In 1971, Esther and Richard bought their current farm in Stockbridge. Richard, who has retired from a full-time job, takes care of the hay, corn, and wheat. Of the six Kapp children, only one, Linda Rogers, looks likely to continue farming. She helps with the family's three greenhouses, and Esther's niece, Lisa Maulbetsch, comes with her to market. Why does Kapp stay with it if the kids aren't going to? "Because I love to grow things," she says.

Kapp is one of few farmers to grow rutabagas. Why has this old-time vegetable practically disappeared from American cuisine? Market-goer Marc Ross conjectures it's because, like cabbage, it became an overused vegetable during World War II, when it was both cheap and overcooked. Another reason may be their physiognomy. "They're so ugly," Kapp admits, "but they're so good." Rutabagas do look awful. They're prone to bugs and they sprout easily. (Another reason for their lack of popularity is that, to counter these problems, grocery stores sell them waxed, which keeps them from breathing and makes their flavor quite strong and acrid.) Unwaxed rutabagas look like cratered, purple, yellow, and white planets. Their texture and flavor are somewhat like a combination of potato and turnip. Boiled and mashed, they are a delicious, piquant alternative to potatoes. Peeled and wiped with oil, they are also good roasted, alone or with other winter root vegetables. ➤

TIPS

If you're going to use just part of an onion, don't cut off the root end. Doing so makes the leftover part taste hot. "You can taste the difference after just a few minutes," Esther Kapp says. "Just start cutting from the top, and keep the rest in a plastic bag in the refrigerator."

Tomatoes ripen from the center out, so they can be ripened in a paper bag or other dark place.

You can freeze whole onions by just putting them in a plastic bag. They do not adhere to each other, so it's easy to remove one or two when needed.

Tomatoes, when frozen whole, easily shed their skins under warm running water.

"Corn should be steamed for only three minutes," Esther Kapp says. **"I put it in one inch of boiling water in a heavy kettle or Dutch oven—it can be heaped up. Put on the cover and steam for just three minutes. The longer you cook it, the tougher it gets. And you should never add salt."**

Esther Kapp puts up "dilly beans" by steaming green beans, then canning them in a broth of vinegar, hot water, and dill. (They're delicious in salads, and a piquant alternative to the olive in a martini.)

Esther Kapp dries herbs by simply placing them in flat baskets. She puts them out when the sun is shining and takes them in when it's not. It takes a couple of weeks depending on how much the sun shines, she says.

Kohlrabi, another old-fashioned veggie not well known to urban cooks, is somewhat like a combination of cabbage and turnip. Kapp uses it raw on a relish tray, grated into salad, or boiled and eaten with salt, pepper, and butter. She finds the new varieties of eggplant to be better than old ones. She grills the long, slim Italian ones with the skin on or uses them in casseroles.

That October morning she had big, lush bunches of curly kale. "I boil it with smoked meat, like Polish sausage, potatoes, and onions for about twenty minutes," she says. Or you can boil it alone and then add a little vinegar and salt; or you can use it like a piece of lettuce on a sandwich." ◯

AL AND FLORENCE KIERCZAK

Al and Florence Kierczak grew up just a few miles apart in Milan. They met and married in 1949, but it wasn't until 1986, when they took a trip to Poland, that they learned that their parents had grown up within a few miles of each other, in Andrychow, a small town in southern Poland. Several of the young people helping out in the Kierczaks' three booths, near the busiest corner of the market, are their nieces and nephews—the offspring of the marriages of Florence's two sisters to Al's two brothers! This truly close-knit family shares an ethic of hard work, which translates to exceptional quality, presentation, and good will.

Al Kierczak (it's short for Albion), began coming to the Ann Arbor City Market when it was located on the grounds of the old courthouse at the corner of Main and Ann. He came as a helper to his father, Michael, who had arrived from Poland in 1912. Al remembers his father saying the family wouldn't have made it through the Depression without their market income. Michael Kierczak played polkas on the button accordion. Al does, too. He taught himself, sneaking the accordion out of the closet when his dad was away from the house.

When Michael died at the age of forty-two, Al, who even then sported his signature pencil-slim mustache, took over the farming. For a long time the family grew corn, wheat, and soybeans on 600 acres, in addition to their market garden. Now, Florence and Al garden twenty acres of vegetables and flowers to bring to the Farmers' Market. With profits dropping out of farming, Al wonders about the future for all market gardeners.

"We don't charge that much more than we did twenty years ago," Kierczak said one recent early July. "Those beans are a dollar and a quarter a box because they're the first, but in a couple of weeks, they'll be a dollar. There used to be a celery man, an onion man, a carrot man. Now we do them all. I do something most of the young people don't do today—I bunch them." On this July day, the Kierczaks' table looked like the working side of a tapestry. The greens (mustard and turnip greens, collard, kale, Swiss chard) mingled with tidy bunches of carrots, scallions, and beets tapering into tiny threadlike tips that look like the delicate ends of a master weaver's yarns.

Al and Florence, and whichever nieces and nephews are helping out, get up at 2:30 a.m. on market days. They'll have stayed up until almost midnight the preceding night, washing and bunching the produce and loading it on the truck. It's worth it, he said. "It's beautiful at the market in the morning. You should come see."

We asked Kierczak lots of questions about how the seasons, the weather, his farm's soil, and his customers' requests affect the varieties of seed he chooses and the farming techniques he uses. On that beautiful Wednesday in early July, we looked at the Kierczaks' produce as we talked. Here are some of his comments, grouped together: "My cabbage—there's no spray on it. You can eat every leaf. I don't use any deadly sprays on anything. ➤

FARM RECIPE

"Take sweet Italian peppers. Chop them up and sauté them," Al Kierczak says. Add eggs and make scrambled eggs. You can put a little jalapeño in there if you want them hot. People love it."

TIP

"You shouldn't boil soft summer squashes," Al Kierczak says. "That takes everything out of them. Just take a little oleo or butter and sauté them a few minutes, and they're done."

My potatoes are sand-grown. If you grow them on clay, they'll be all scabbed. We harvest them by hand. The ones at the store are picked by a harvester—that's what gives them those black [bruise] spots. For tomatoes, you want loam or heavier ground. It's no use putting seed in before the ground is sixty-five degrees. [Otherwise] it won't come up. I have some of my plants started in a greenhouse. They're absolutely gorgeous when I plant them.

"These are early potatoes. The white ones are Onaways, from Onaway, Michigan; they're good for mashed. The red ones are Norland; they don't fall apart in potato salad. We wash them. We wash everything. We dump them on a screen, hose them, and grade them." For the last eight to ten years, the Kierczaks have been bringing miniature vegetables to market. "These are Nantes carrots," Kierczak said. "They're one of the sweetest and one of the oldest and still the best. I try to pick them small. I plant them thick so they won't grow big. Provider is a nice meaty bean. Next, I'll have Derby beans; they do a little better in hot weather.

"I've disked the lettuce and peas under. I had three kinds of peas—early, ten days later, and then a few days later. Now I'll plant pickles [pickling cucumbers] and summer squash. I plant four varieties of cucumbers because the pollination does better when they're mixed." The Kierczaks' booth is one of the rare places where fresh pimientos can be found. Kierczak doesn't know why they're so uncommon, though he did say they're harder to grow.

"We have about 160,000 glad bulbs. We'll have blooms from July through September," he said. They also grow zinnias, snapdragons, and dark red cockscomb, which Kierczak calls "an old-fashioned flower"; but peonies are his favorite. "I've got some new ones coming," he said happily. "They cost up to sixty dollars a root—ten to sixty dollars—but they last about twenty years. I had a florist come last year, wanted to buy all of them, but I wouldn't [let him]. I wanted some for my other customers, too."

What do the Kierczaks do with the leftovers at the end of market day? That's easy. There aren't any. ◯

KITCHEN PORT

Wok, couscousière, quiche pan, daikon shredder, sushi mat, aebleskiver pan, spaetzle press, tortilla press. Before the middle of the twentieth century, what home cook, or even professional chef, could have been familiar with them all? An Italian chef had a pasta dryer; a French chef had a mandolin; a Chinese chef had a bamboo steamer, and so on. But now any customer at the Farmers' Market is likely to have an international array of pots, pans, stirrers, steamers, mashers, grinders, sprayers, pickers, pokers, and what not. It's hard to remember that only thirty years ago these items were extremely rare in American kitchens. In Ann Arbor, the 1969 opening of Kitchen Port was a turning point. From the beginning, the store has carried exotic as well as more traditional American equipment and has been staffed with enthusiastic cooks who generously share their knowledge.

Frustrated by the difficulty of finding top quality kitchenware, local lawyer Art Carpenter and a group of friends put together the idea for the store. (It was the first step of a grander plan that included the opening of Kerrytown two years later.) To raise capital, they all became shareholders. Carpenter's law office was in the wedge-shaped Arbor A building across North Fifth Avenue from the Farmers' Market. The building's basement was empty, and it looked like a good and inexpensive place to begin.

Busy with his law practice, Carpenter had to find a store manager. Ricky Agranoff (co-author of this book), already a well-established cook and cooking teacher, was a clear and, fortunately, willing choice. Current Kitchen Port manager Roberta Shrope has been involved with the store since 1977. One Monday afternoon in February, Ricky, Roberta, general merchandise manager Amy Winchester, and I got together in the Kitchen Port office and talked about old times and new. The store's basic premise hasn't changed at all.

"The idea was to have the best quality goods across a broad range—heirloom quality things that people could pass on in their families," Ricky said. "We took ten thousand dollars of shareholder money, and Art and I went to New York on a big buying trip. We wanted quality and variety. Before that, only people involved in gourmet cooking knew where to buy things. I guess most kitchen equipment came from the hardware store and from home parties, like cutlery parties. We wanted to sell the best quality across the board—for people who couldn't pay very much and for people who could. We were open to the community and we had a demo kitchen. In the early Seventies we moved to a downstairs place in the Kerrytown buildings, and a few years later we moved upstairs."

In 1992 Kitchen Port opened a second store at Traver Village shopping center on Ann Arbor's north side and in 1998 another in Brighton, MI. The Kerrytown store remains the hub; it still does kitchen demonstrations on Wednesdays from noon to 1 p.m. and offers cooking classes on Thursdays from 6:30 to 8:30 p.m. And it still answers cooking questions galore. The afternoon we were there, Amy said she had answered many telephone queries already that day. What kinds of questions? "Well," she said, "someone wanted to know about cooking with aluminum. She was worried about interaction with tomatoes, but the anodized aluminum cookware we sell doesn't interact with acidic foods."

From the time Kitchen Port opened, it had a strong relationship with the Ann Arbor Farmers' Market, which means a lot to Roberta. "I've been associated with the market all my life," she told us. "My grandparents had a hog and chicken farm in Dixboro. My grandmother made clothes for me out of feed sacks we purchased when this building housed a granary. They sold chickens at the market. I remember hanging out there. People like the excitement of the market. We're all intimately connected. The chain of events in keeping food fresh and preserving it has changed—the milkman came to your door, there was not one big grocery store or little Asian markets. That affects the Farmers' Market and the way people cook. For example, we have a lot of glass containers and anti-bacterial cutting boards now, because people are very conscious of safety. Amy keeps track of consumer trends—people expect us to know."

The relationship of the market and Kitchen Port echoes back and forth symbiotically. As customers ask the growers for Chinese greens and Thai lemongrass, they also ask the shop for proper cooking equipment and more cookbooks. "We choose products for the best performance in each category," Amy said. "For example, we have Wusthof Trident knives because they're a fair price for the quality and the company warranties them. So we've had twenty- and thirty-year-old knives come in that we've been able to get warranty service for." Under the direction of Jane West, Kitchen Port's cookbook section has expanded over the last three years. "Jane has a knack for getting the right book," Roberta said. "It's a gift she has."

If Kitchen Port has a problem, it's that sometimes people perceive it to be more expensive than national stores that advertise specials, but Roberta and Amy say their everyday prices are comparable to those specials. To that, customers can add the extra value of patient and thorough advice and service. It's also the one-stop place to get anything from Pyrex casseroles to salad bowls to bread machines. The store has a fascinating wall of kitchen gadgets, heavy country pottery, glassware, fabulous pots and pans—Calphalon anodized aluminum, All-Clad stainless steel, Le Crueset cast iron, etc.—coffee and tea brewing wares, complete fancy baking supplies, and even small garden supplies for herb and salad enthusiasts. ○

TINA KOSKI

"I'm known as the pepper lady," says Tina Koski. "I grow thirteen kinds of peppers—they range from jalapeños, which are medium green and very hot," she explains, "through anchos, which are dark green and medium hot, to Anaheim, which are light green and milder. [They're often used for chiles rellenos]. I also grow sweet peppers. For the last three or four years I've been growing purple ones. They have about the same taste as my red ones, and I have yellow ones which are a little sweeter. Some ladies buy by the bushel for salsa."

Koski is one member of the extended family that includes her sister Delores Gracia, her sister-in-law Carol Vena, and her niece Devena Rohn. Koski's stall is next to Gracia's at the busiest corner of the market. Marketing is her way of life. She began helping her parents, Louise and Bessie Vena, with their market booths at Detroit markets when she was a teenager, almost forty years ago. Strong and industrious, she maintains her Ann Arbor Farmers' Market stall every Saturday and Wednesday and goes to the Northville market on Thursdays.

Koski follows the cycle of the year as faithfully as her plants do. In the spring, she sells bedding plants she has helped grow at the Gracia Greenhouse. They include the pepper, tomato, squash, and other veggie starters that she transplants to her own fields in June, and from which she harvests the produce to sell through summer and up through first frost. Then she goes to work as head of a six-woman crew, working from 6 a.m. to midnight, assembling Christmas greens (white pine, cedar, and boxwood) and wreaths for sale at market up to Christmas time. After Christmas, it's back to Gracia's Greenhouse to work on next spring's starter plants. "I play in dirt all the time," she says.

During the height of the season, from July through August, Koski sells several kinds of tomatoes, including large cherry tomatoes and the less acidic small yellow tomatoes. She usually has five or six kinds of squash—green zucchini, yellow summer, white Lebanese, patty pan, and roly poly. "Zucchini," she says, "you can stand around and watch it grow." Like other growers at the market, Koski has added lots of "weird stuff." For the last few years she's been selling squash blossoms, by special request. The blossoms, and the recently popular baby squash, are poor earners. It takes a lot of hand-picked baby squash and even more hand-picked blossoms to equal the yield of just four big squash; but people aren't willing to pay an equally disproportionate price. Koski sells them anyhow because they generate faithful customers. ○

HARVEST STEW

Toina Koski says all the market growers are familiar with what they call "Harvest Stew." "You take what peppers, tomatoes, onions, cabbage, squash, or other vegetables you have," she says. "Wash and chop them to bite size. Throw it all in a pot. Cover it. Let it simmer two or three hours, or put it in a slow cooker. The longer it slow cooks, the more it blends. You could put in celery if you want something that stays more chunky. It could be meat or no meat. (I could be a vegetarian real easy.)"

LEONARD AND GRACE KRUEGER

Come deep summer, Leonard Krueger will get out his garlic sorting box. It's a shallow, weather-worn wooden box divided into sections. A ritzy fabric store could use this antique as a trendy display case to hold fancy buttons, or perhaps a serious woodworker could use it to sort and hold various sizes of screws. Krueger uses it to hold meticulously sorted garlic: individual cloves, multiple cloves, little bulbs, big bulbs, etc. Prices run from six for $1 for single cloves up to $1 for a full bulb, depending on size. Krueger's respectful appraisal of each modest crescent-shaped clove and lumpy bulb is typical of his craftsmanly approach to growing, storing, and marketing produce and flowers.

Most regular market shoppers would recognize gregarious vendors like Florence Kierczak, Tina Koski, and her sister Delores Gracia anywhere, but few would recognize Krueger if they passed him on the street. Many shoppers see him as a crusty, quiet person intent on his own business. But for the few who try to strike up a conversation and to peer under the bill of his farm cap, there's the wonderful surprise: a handsome, craggy, grandfatherly man eager enough to share his knowledge despite the difficulties posed by a hearing aid.

Like the man himself, Krueger's displays are more low-key than most. Tabletops at bigger stalls are heavily laden for a bountiful look. Krueger's single-table displays are spare and simple. A small pile of fresh onions here, ten or so boxes of curly garlic stems there, a few boxes of glowing red currents several inches away. But under the table, kept cool in the shade there, are pails of round white onions kept fresh in a small amount of water. Krueger tends his produce as tenderly, thriftily, and skillfully when it's out of the ground as when it's in. He learned this as a child.

"It will interest you to know," he says, "that my grandfather was in the produce business. He had an orchard, and between him and my mother they grew onions, radishes, carrots, beets, and all. He would take them in a wagon with horses to Adrian [from the Krueger family farm in Blissfield]. It was about ten miles and took two and a half to three hours. He'd start from home at three a.m. and peddle produce house to house. He would go to certain customers up and down the streets." Krueger's sense of history runs deep. He's proud to say that, in ancient geologic time, his good sandy loam was part of the bed of Lake Erie.

Mid-century, this land produced sugar beets, and Krueger's father worked in the sugar factory. But Krueger followed his grandfather's path. His youngest son, Mark, is carrying on the family farming tradition in addition to holding a full-time job as a mold setter at an auto parts manufacturing company in Adrian. Mark and his young son, Kory, grow black radishes, pumpkins, and turnips for the market.

The Krueger family farm (there are actually two now—one for Leonard and Grace and one for Mark's young family) is a little closer to Toledo than to Ann Arbor, so the Kruegers began selling there. But about thirty years ago, they found they were running surpluses so they added an Ann Arbor stall. Soon Ann Arbor profits outstripped those in Toledo and the Kruegers made a permanent switch. Grace Krueger suffered a back injury a few years ago, so Leonard comes alone.

We talked to Krueger in July, before the garlic bulbs were ready but while the green garlic stems were at their peak. Garlic plants are beautiful, visually as well as aromatically. Used in a flower garden, the green stems add a linear effect. They are long, smooth, and more slender than scallion greens. When the seed pod at the top of a stem is full, it looks like a goose's head with a long green beak; often the stems curl, giving the terrific decorative effect of nodding goose heads. (The plants probably ward off some garden pests, but as self-sowers they can themselves become a nuisance.) Krueger harvests the pods, each containing between fourteen to sixteen little sets from which to start new garlic plants. He sells the cut greens for use in stir-fry recipes and stews. The Kruegers also refrigerate the stems in olive oil, to preserve their color and flavor throughout the winter.

Alongside the garlic stems, Krueger that day had boxes of Stark Brothers Gold cherries, mingling the subtle reds and yellows of a Monet painting. Why does he choose to grow that variety of early cherries? "Because," he says, "they don't look like they're ripe, so they kind of fool the birds, see? So they don't start in on these until the others are gone." Can customers tell the difference between these and red July cherries? Not blindfolded," Krueger says, succinctly.

A customer stops to ask what the funny goosebumpy looking berries are. "Mulberries," Krueger tells her. "They're not native to this country. They were introduced here from China for silkworms."

"We moved here from Vermont," the customer says. "There are a lot more varieties here. We had a farmers' market in Vermont, but it was just so-so produce at a very high price." She buys a box of cherries and a box of mulberries. She'll make up a pie recipe to suit them, she says.

As the summer goes along, Krueger says, he'll have beans, squash, kohlrabi, parsnips, cabbage, onions, Brussels sprouts, tomatoes, and more. In early spring he brings horseradish root and French pussy willows. Despite this great range, Krueger is known to many customers as "the garlic man." To a few very specialized customers, though, he's known as "the black walnut man." Black walnuts, which have a stronger flavor than the English walnuts sold in stores, are extremely difficult to shell and thus are all but unavailable. It takes a patient husbandman like Leonard Krueger to bring them to market. First he has to soak the nuts, still encased in their green outer hulls, in a tub of water. Next he drills a hole in each one and patiently removes the softened hull. Then he has to remove the hard woody shell and extricate the fragrant nut. He regrets the price of a package—$8 for a large cupful—but each package takes him between two and a half and three hours to produce. So the rare and highly prized nuts can still fairly be called a bargain. ○

MERKEL GARDENS
GEORGE & NANCY MERKEL
AND FAMILY

Wet or dry,

plant your turnips

around the twenty-first of July.

A cold and wet May

will fill your barn

with grain and hay.

We went to visit the Merkels at their Chelsea home because Nancy Merkel has Parkinson's disease and it's hard for her to get out. Her husband, George, good-humoredly recited for us some of the little farm jingles he remembers his father, Joe, teaching him. George's family has been farming in the Chelsea area west of Ann Arbor since the 1880's. So has Nancy's, and she has come to the Ann Arbor Farmers' Market since infancy. Her parents, Leon and Clarice Clark, were early participants in the market. "Mr. Dieterle [one of the market's revered old-timers] remembers laying me on the front seat of the truck," she recalls, her eyes twinkling. Though Nancy finds it too difficult to go to market with George now, she's still active in Merkel Gardens. In the spring she sells flower baskets—about 1,000 of them. "I'm known as 'the flower lady' in Chelsea," she says. Many older Ann Arborites may also remember Nancy as the Union Bar lady. From 1962 to 1972, Nancy and George owned the restaurant and bar at the corner of West Liberty and Ashley that is now the Old Town.

Two of the Merkels' seven children, Margaret Stech and Ann Salyer, plan to carry on the family farm business. Farm activity in the area is decreasing rapidly as land is subdivided "into ten-acre parcels where they're building huge houses," Nancy says from her homey dining room. That's less of a problem for small truck farmers than for farmers who grow soybeans or feed corn as cash crops to sell to the grain elevator. "Ten acres is a heck of a lot of land for growing vegetables," George says. "Ten acres of soybeans is nothing." The Merkel family owns and rents a number of small parcels, and they believe it will be possible to keep up profitable truck farming. They have backup, however, in the full-time jobs held by Margaret and Ann's husbands, Bill and Rod.

Do farmers worry a lot about being wiped out by weather, insects, and such? "Most farmers do, but he doesn't," Nancy says, smiling at George.

"I figure if I grow enough things, something will work," George adds. He starts his own seed in the basement in deep winter, and moves the seedlings to his greenhouse a month later. In addition to old standards like beans, cauliflower, broccoli, and tomatoes, the Merkels have been growing Chinese vegetables and melons. They began when Nancy's nephew married a Korean woman who brought them seed.

As the young women take on more and more of the farming responsibilities, George will increasingly move into his new hobby of restoring antique tractors along with Ann's husband, Rod. Tractors that sold for between $500 and $600 when new in the 1930's to the 1950's can fetch between $5,000 and $6,000 as showpieces today.

The Merkels' market stall also provides a way for Margaret to indulge a new hobby. She showed us a pan full of flowers she'd recently dried in the microwave oven—equipment and directions for doing this, she says, are available at stores like Michael's and Frank's. She'll use the flowers she grew and dried to create table decorations and wreaths that she'll take to market up until Christmas time.

"My dad sold potatoes door-to-door in Ann Arbor," George told us. "People used to buy five to ten bushels to last them through the winter. Now people buy by the peck" (a quarter of a bushel). And then, as if to prove that the world hasn't changed as much as George was implying, someone came onto the front porch.

"It's the Schwan's man," said Margaret. Schwan's is a national company selling food products door-to-door. Unlike, George Merkel's potatoes, Schwan's potatoes are already cooked, mashed, and preserved in nuggets, and Schwan's products are frozen, so a home-maker can still stock up for the winter. It's a boon for Nancy, who, with grandchildren in the neighborhood, likes to have Schwan's pizzas in the freezer. She placed her order as Margaret left to pick tomatoes to take to market the next day. ◯

TIP

Of the several types of string beans, Nancy Merkel prefers the purple ones. When cooked, they turn a deep green. "I think they're the best tasting," she says, "and they make a pretty bean to freeze."

MERRY BERRY FARM
JIM AND MARYANN BREMMER

It's not a surprise to learn that the grower who dresses like a Disneyland farm hand, and whose home is called Merry Berry Farm, has a whopping sense of humor. Somehow it is a surprise to learn that Jim Bremmer is a retired state trooper and detective sergeant. While still in his official uniform (rather than his self-imposed market get-up that includes wide bright red suspenders and what looks like an Amish hat), Bremmer and his wife, MaryAnn, maintained a big garden at home. Jim retired from the force in 1982 and turned to teaching at high school and college, while enlarging the family garden into a small farm. Output was soon big enough for the Bremmers to take a stall at the Adrian market, with an eventual move to the larger Ann Arbor Farmers' Market.

When he first came to Ann Arbor, Jim wore his black, Western-style felt hat in the traditional manner, with the top creased down. One day he happened to push the crown up preparatory to folding in the crease, and just never quite finished. The crown stayed up in the manner of the Amish. People noticed. He heard one shopper ask another where she got her jar of honey and the reply was, "From the man with the tall black hat." He'd accidentally created an advertising gimmick that tickled his funny bone and was comfortable besides. "So," he says, "I've been stuck with this sucker ever since." A big man, with his big white beard, red suspenders, the hat, baggy blue jeans, and blunt-toed black work boots, Bremmer looks like a mythic kindly man—a combined Santa Claus and highly moral farmer.

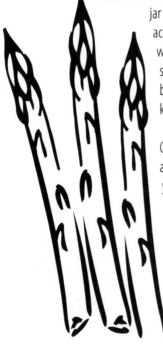

Maybe an aura of a trooper's protectiveness shines around him too. Customers confide in Bremmer. The day we interviewed him, he was polishing apples to a high shine with a green-and-white-striped terry cloth. A youngish man came up and asked which apples would be best for a pie. "Right now you can use Macs," Bremmer replied. "They're still crisp and tart. Later they get softer and sweeter." He bagged some up. More conversation ensued. It turned out that this was to be the abashed customer's first attempt at a pie. Bremmer unbagged the apples. "Let me give you the larger size," he advised, "so you won't have to peel so much."

A toddler passing by reached reflexively to Bremmer's basket of polished apples, but her mother, not noticing, tugged her on. "Wait," said the observant Bremmer. "I have a child-sized apple in here." He searched around in the basket and popped a little apple into the toddler's hand. She looked confused. The ex-trooper realized he was not only a stranger, but a huge and rather strange stranger. He handed an adult-size apple to the mom. Then, beaming, the little girl trustingly held up her apple and said, "Mine."

A woman looking at Bremmer's jars of golden honey asked how to get started in bee culture. "You go buy you a bee colony," Bremmer answered with exaggerated innocence, "and you get a book and you start reading . . ."

Merry Berry Farms got into the bee business in order to ensure pollination. Mites in this area, Bremmer says, have resulted in huge losses of wild bees. Although the problem seems to be ebbing, the Bremmers will keep their hives. Many of his customers, he says, say honey protects them from allergies because ingesting tiny amounts of pollen-derived food may help the body develop natural immunity. "Whether it's psychological or an actual fact, I can't say," Bremmer explains, "but if it works, that's great."

Merry Berry begins the market year with asparagus in early spring. That's followed by strawberries, then the huge crops of summer, followed by the apples and ever-bearing raspberries they bring both spring and fall. For the last few years, the Bremmers have been selling chickens to customers who order them in advance. What does Bremmer do in the winter? "Fix the things I break in the summer," he says. Then deciding the impertinence is too great for his gentle style, he adds, "No, really—there's always a lot to do." ○

MONAHAN'S SEAFOOD MARKET
MIKE MONAHAN

Monahan's Seafood Market is to fish as Tiffany's is to jewelry. At both places, the product is perfectly cut and sparkly. Where the existence of diamonds depends upon violent pressures of ancient rock, the existence of fish depends on the moisture and flexibility of buoyant seas; the skill in both cases is to retain nature's gift through careful handling and craftsmanship. Unlike the grocery stores served by mass-market distribution systems, Monahan's market staff handles seafood delicately enough to deliver all its value to his customers.

"The flavor, goodness, and nutrition is in the fat and moisture of the fish," says Mike Monahan. As a master of his trade, Monahan has a lot to say about what keeps fish fresh and full of "goodness." Methods of handling, from the way the fish are caught to how they're wrapped, affect the way they ultimately reach the table. For example, Monahan says, fish caught in gill nets struggle in the nets, which releases glycogen, softening the flesh. More expensive methods, such as "long line" fishing or harpoon fishing, which bring in big fish like swordfish one at a time, retain their top condition.

Another big divergence takes place at the dock, where a trusted buyer picks fish according to Monahan's specifications. Fishing boats, Monahan says, often are at sea for two weeks. During that time, they accumulate piles of fish and ice that ultimately weigh many tons. "Somebody gets the top [of the pile]," Monahan says, "and somebody gets the bottom. It all gets sold, and we get the top of the catch."

"When you see swordfish, say, for seven ninety-five a pound," he says, "and other swordfish for seventeen ninety-five a pound, it's an entirely different product. One may be gill-netted imported swordfish, while the other may be a fresh domestic swordfish that's nice and fat and full of flavor. We don't buy imported swordfish because they may be gill-netted and because the travel time is too long and the handling may be poor. Since we're in the middle of the country, we don't have the regional bias that the coastal towns have; we buy the best from the whole country and can sell it to Ann Arbor's diverse community. That's why we have one of the best selections in the country. We really do. Also, we buy whole fish and cut them here. As soon as a fish is exposed to air, it starts to lose moisture; but most fish counters sell pre-cut fillets."

Although some fine fish is expensive, Monahan says in-season fish are always a best buy—low in price and high in flavor. And Monahan's knowledgeable staff is as friendly and helpful as he is and can work with a customer to make a moderately priced but special fish dinner. "For example, we'll put together a fruit of the sea mix," he says, "with Manila clams, a couple of shrimp, some nice Atlantic squid. You cook it with some white wine, garlic, and olive oil and serve it on pasta for a great meal.

"No matter what, I'd want to be involved in the fish business in some way," he says. "It's a fun and interesting business. There is no more wonderful and diverse food in the world. It changes seasonally, and there's always something at its peak that you didn't have the month before.

"I've always been a sports fisherman. I was raised on Lake Saint Clair, and I've lived and fished in Connecticut and Florida. I came back to Ann Arbor in 1975 and worked as a free-lance artist and then for a moving company, but I hurt my back. So I got a part-time job at the Real Seafood Market at Kerrytown. Paul [Saginaw—now co-owner of Zingerman's] was working at Cafe Creole [a former restaurant that was located on Catherine, a block from the Farmers' Market]. We'd been friends for a long time. We talked about buying the fish market from Paul's employers, the people at the Real Seafood restaurant on Main Street. This was the only [fish] place in town.

"We thought we could do things that they weren't doing. They weren't selling many whole fish or catering to the ethnic market. We tried to bring in everything. We doubled the business in the first year. We still cater to all the groups in Ann Arbor. We always try new things. You never stop learning.

"In the spring there is shad—people from Calcutta request it—and shad roe for transplanted easterners, especially people from the Chesapeake Bay area. Arctic Maine shrimp, or 'ama ebi,' which means sweet shrimp, is eaten raw or sauteed by the Japanese; Chinese cooks steam black sea bass from Rhode Island; British Columbian Manila clams, 'asari' in Japanese, are similar to a Mediterranean clam. The Italians cook them with garlic, parsley, and white wine to serve over spaghetti, and the Spaniards use them in paella. Belgians come in for Mediterranean sea mussels farm-raised in Washington, which are so high in meat-to-shell ratio they look like they're trying to escape their shells.

"We've always been a cook's market," Monahan adds, meaning that most of his customers spend a fair amount of time cooking. "But the times dictate the need for convenient, easy-to-cook food." So he's been making meals that are ready to cook or microwave. Many are wrapped in parchment, ready to pop into the microwave or regular oven. For example, Tilapia San Remo is a tilapia fillet combined with farm butter, sun-dried tomatoes, chives, white wine, and grated Parmesan Reggiano cheese and wrapped in parchment paper. Baked for twelve minutes, it's ready to serve. (For customers who want to prepare their own, Monahan's even provides free parchment paper.)

Monahan's also has a case of smoked seafood products, many kinds of marinated herring, cooked shrimp, fish pâtés, house-cured gravlax, and seafood salads. ◯

ALEX AND AGNES NEMETH

Alex Nemeth tucked down his chin and laughed when we asked him how we could tell whether the melons we buy from him are ripe or not. "We never bring ones that aren't ripe," he said, amused at the very idea. "The ones in the supermarket, though—they're always picked green."

It was so cold on the January Saturday we met with him, that we retreated to the Market offices. That's when we found out that during the winter, the few farmers that continue to come to the market take turns bringing pots full of food for all to share. It happened to be Alex and Agnes Nemeth's turn, and they had supplied a pot of bean soup and one of chicken soup.

An archetypal farmer, Nemeth, a burly, handsome man, often wears plaid flannel shirts and, of course, a billed cap, and he isn't a big talker. But he kindly and patiently told us about the pleasures and problems of fruit farming in this area. His parents emigrated from Hungary to Detroit. In 1931, they bought the present eighty-acre Nemeth family farm in Ypsilanti. Alex came to the market for the first time in 1932. He was a year old.

He remembers the market when it had a wooden plank floor instead of the current concrete. He remembers eating breakfast at the Biederman house. Since razed, it stood on North Fourth Avenue on ground that is now part of the market parking lot. The Biederman family lived in the house and served meals on market days. When you got in your parents' way, Nemeth recalls, they'd say, "Just go over to Biederman's." He remembers farmers with horse-drawn carts bringing corn to the grist mill in what is now the Kerry-town Market Building. And he recalls a period in the 1930's when "two little old ladies came to market in battery-powered cars." The restaurant across South Fifth from the market, now DeLong's Barbecue, was named the Elbow Room because, as Nemeth explained, if you ate there, you hardly had room to bend your elbows.

"Our light soil is suited for an orchard," he said. "Fruit gets better flavor when it's grown in lighter soils. Heavier soils are good for grain." Western Michigan has a lot of sandy Lake Michigan soil and is good fruit-farming country. Much of that fruit is sold for processing. Smaller-scale fruit farmers in this area usually sell at local markets and fruit stands. Agnes joined Alex at the market after they were married in 1952. They bring apples, apple cider, caramel apples, peaches, pears, and grapes.

They raise about twenty-seven varieties of apples, including old standbys like Jonathan, Delicious, Macintosh, Winesap, and Spy. Jonathans remain Nemeth's favorites for their tart flavor, crisp bite, and because they're good for cider and caramel apples. He cited Gala as an apple whose flesh and skin blend together.

The Nemeths make cider every Friday from early October until April. They use a blend of apples—"five bushels of this, five bushels of that," is how Alex puts it.

From time to time they grow new varieties. The payoff for a new tree is quicker than it used to be. A new dwarf tree, Nemeth said, can bear apples in as few as four years—lots faster than traditional varieties that usually require eight years to bear. On the other hand, a semi-dwarf tree may last only about twenty years. The Nemeth orchards include some bearing trees that are thought to be eighty-five years old.

The Nemeths trim their trees between December and mid-April. Pruning and thinning is necessary, Nemeth said, because if the tree gets too dense, "the apples don't size up right," and if the sun can't reach through, "they don't get good flavor." Peaches begin with Condor, ripe in mid-July. Red Havens take over between the end of July and the middle of August. They're good for canning because they don't discolor and their pit comes loose easily. Fragile Pink Champagnes (known as "white peaches") are available for only a few days, generally during the first week of August.

Pears include the old favorite, Bartletts, and a larger, longer-lasting mutation called Spartletts. The Nemeths have both purple and green grapes—Concords and Niagaras. In late summer, they also bring sweet corn and muskmelon.

We talked some about the future of farming. Clearly the family is optimistic—Agnes and Alex's son Robert is now a fruit grower, too, and also has a stall at the market. However, Nemeth confirms that it's harder than it used to be. Expenses including taxes and insurance are higher, there are more regulations and associated paperwork to attend to, and land becomes increasingly valuable for developers.

The proof? "Between our place and Ypsilanti, there used to be twenty-five farms," Nemeth said. "Now what? Three?

"It costs a lot of money and work to make cider now [because of new regulations]. Luckily, we built a new storage building in Eighty-five with a separate room for making cider." Despite increased costs, when they began milling cider in the 1950's they sold it for $1 a gallon; it's $4 a gallon now, which means that its price, in 1950 dollars, has probably gone down! Moreover, customers buy produce in smaller quantities now. They used to buy in bushels; now it's small bags. That, Nemeth says, means that a grower needs more than one stall and more help to make enough sales to keep going. With cider a year-round crop, he said, "we haven't missed a winter in ten years."

Though he hadn't thought about it before, he estimated that he probably sells to 600 customers on July and August Saturdays, and about 200 on December Saturdays. What else does he do in winter? "I have a [work]shop," he said. "I make chairs, tables, rocking horses, hope chests, trellises . . . . We have hardwood trees. It's a good use for the wood." His output is for gifts, he said, when we finally asked a question he really liked. "We have," he answered, "five kids and fourteen grandchildren." ⭕

KARL NEUVIRTH

At the height of the season, Karl Neuvirth sells 300 dozen ears of corn by one o'clock every Saturday afternoon. Neuvirth is continuing a family tradition. His parents, Karl and Mary, opened a greenhouse during the Depression. They began selling at the Ann Arbor Farmers' Market in the early 1950's at the same stall Karl uses now. He inherited the greenhouse about twenty years ago and renamed it the Oakville Greenhouse. He runs it while also working at a full-time job. "I wouldn't do it [have a job] if it wasn't for making a living and insurance and everything," he says. He's looking forward to retiring in a few years and becoming a full-time grower. In the meantime he works from 6 a.m. to 9 p.m. seven days a week. Of his five children, one, his thirty-one-year-old son, Kris, farms with him. "We operate as a family deal," Karl says happily. Besides selling at the Ann Arbor Farmers' Market, the Newvirths own a store called Oakville Greenhouse and Produce, located at the corner of US-23 and Carpenter Road in Milan.

The largest portion of Neuvirth's market sales are bedding plants and potted plants from the Oakville Greenhouse. Throughout the summer he brings "a few tomatoes, beans . . . depends how hard I want to work," he says. But there's no doubt that come August, Neuvirth will be at the market with a truckload of corn. He reserves forty acres just for corn, planting every week or ten days so the crop comes in fresh all through the season; then, forgoing irrigation or other watering, he says, "I just let nature take care of itself." The delicate variety he plants is very tender and has to be picked by hand. "Corn is the easiest," he says. "Tomatoes, you have to pick and hope people don't squeeze them all. We used to bring white corn; now we grow the yellow and white. It's the best in the market. Corn is better than it used to be [thanks to hybrids]. It used to get starchy after a few hours. Now, she'll hold for twenty-four hours." ○

PARTNERS IN WINE AND CHEESE
KARL JOHNSON

These days, to owner Karl Johnson, the name Partners in Wine and Cheese designates a partnership between customers and knowledgeable staff members as well as the natural partnership of wine and cheese. In 1982, with four investing partners, Johnson opened Partners in Wine at South Main Market. There have been many changes in the group over the years. By 1985, the then-partners opened Partners in Wine and Cheese at Kerrytown. The new, longer name expressed Johnson's interest in emphasizing the relationship between fine food and wine. Five years ago, Johnson sold his share of the Main Street shop. Now, although Ann Arbor still has two stores with similar names and a shared early history, each one has evolved to match its owners' styles and interests.

"I focus on wine and cheese and on doing wine and food consultation," Johnson says. "I have over fifteen hundred wines. I taste each wine—each vintage. I try not to carry brand names— the big companies with heavy advertising who are trying to control the market. Though I lean toward the wines of Italy, France, Spain, South Africa, and Michigan, select wines from California, Australia, and South America can be wonderful." He personally knows the owners and vintners of the eighteen or so established Michigan Wineries.

He chooses wine primarily for taste and effect, but also for value. For example, he pointed out a Languedoc-Rousillon, selling at $7.99 a bottle at the time of our conversation, that compares quite well to a Rhone at $15. Both, he says, are full-bodied, dark, spicy, and earthy, and both are made from Rhone grapes. Johnson's prices range from $4.99 to $50. He provides additional economies with a 5 percent discount on half cases of wine, and a 12 percent discount on full cases.

Although the dairy case looks small, it holds about 120 cheeses. They include classics like English Farmhouse Cheddar; blues like Stilton and Gorgonzola; aromatics like Limburger and Morbier; and self-ripeners like Taleggio, Brie, and Camembert. The cheeses come from all over the world, and in addition to standards like Parmesan from Italy, the store stocks a range of imported goat's milk and sheep's milk cheeses, including Bucheron from France, kasseri from Greece, and manchego from Spain.

Johnson, though he's in his fifties and a twenty-six-year veteran of the business, looks like a curly-haired choir boy—an especially joyful one when he is talking about the flavors and virtues of various wines and suggesting food and wine combinations. "The Languedoc-Rousillon or the Rhone would go well with a zesty dish like bean stew or Italian tomato-based dishes," he says. "I love sheep's cheese, like manchego, in salad and with a good red wine." For dessert he likes to match an apple dish of any kind with a Gewurztraminer, a white wine with a "spicy, crushed-herb quality."

"I like wines," he says, "that support creative dining. The key thing is to pick what's appropriate for the occasion—for you, your guests, and the food."

Partners in Wine and Cheese also carries foods for appetizer plates and even for some entire meals. They have lots of packaged crackers, cookies, oils, jams, soup mixes, drink mixes, pastas, sauces, condiments, freshly roasted coffee beans, and fresh breads and pastries from Ann Arbor and Detroit specialty bakeries.

"I have a favorite recipe using only products from our store, except for the fresh rapini [a relative of broccoli] and tofu," Johnson says. It calls for mushroom fettucini (carried in bags at Partners in Wine and Cheese), sun-dried tomatoes (which the store sells in bulk), pine nuts (in packages), kalamata olives (jars), morels (in packages, dried), roasted red peppers (Johnson sells them in jars, but recommends that cooks roast their own fresh peppers, if possible), rapini florets (sometimes available at Zingerman's Practical Produce) or otherwise broccoli flowers, firm tofu (available at Zingerman's Practical Produce and People's Food Co-op), soy sauce (bottles), and Italian spices (jars, though Johnson recommends fresh spices where possible). The real pizzazz in this recipe is the addition of finely diced moist French goat cheese, which adds fabulous flavor and, appearing as creamy white flecks, visually enlivens the dish as well. Happiness, Johnson suggests, is this dish assembled according to the logic and mood of the chef and served with a Dolcetto d'Alba Piedmont red. ○

PEOPLE'S FOOD CO-OP

The People's Food Co-op, on North Fourth Avenue just half a block south of the Farmers' Market, is the Cinderella of grocery stores: initially, it may seem too sweet, too sincere, too plain, but finally, the shoe fits a reality of substance, quality, and beauty. To folks who haven't been there in the last few years, the idea of the Co-op may evoke images of dusty floors, bruised fruits, and cardboard tasting food. But People's, expanded and renovated in 1994, looks terrific, sells great stuff, and has a lot of ritzy surprises. On our visit there, Ricky quickly spotted favorite products that she usually expects to find only in gourmet food shops. She was delighted to find Callebaut semi-sweet chocolate, French Dupuy lentils, and dried Urbani brand porcini mushrooms—all at reasonable prices.

The lingo in Co-op publications is very unKrogeresque. Instead of stockholders, there are members; instead of glitzy corporate reports, there's an Owner's Manual; instead of profits, there are rights, benefits, and responsibilities; instead of vice-presidents, there's an outreach and education manager, who, when we visited, was Sharon Barbour. We sat and chatted with her at a little round table next to the Co-op's sunny front window. The table is there so people can chat, as we were doing, or look through the Co-op's informational notebooks and scrapbooks, which include free apartment listings, nutrition information, and news about local organic farming.

The purpose of the Co-op, Barbour told us, is to provide consumers with natural foods and other products while promoting nutritional awareness and environmental responsibility. The plan includes working with local organic growers. The Co-op provides a retail outlet for the growers, who through their farms, in turn, protect the remaining green areas around our growing city. So though they're not aware of it, even people who don't shop at the Co-op benefit from it.

Co-op membership is not required of customers. But when we spoke with Barbour, lifetime membership was available for $60, refundable on request. Membership benefits included a 3 percent discount on Co-op purchases and varying discounts at about three dozen other local businesses. Working members currently get a 10 percent discount and make up the majority of the store's staff, which accounts, in part, for the very casual and lively atmosphere. Check-out staff is paid, as is store management.

Just as the product line includes a lot of sophisticated stuff, so does the customer mix. When we were there, a scrawny young man dressed in leather and bearing a variety of earrings, nose rings, and who knows what other rings, and a comfy-looking woman in a white sweatsuit and diamond rings (presumably restricted to her fingers), were studying the same shelf of fruit juices. The downtown location presents a parking problem, but after shopping, customers can drive up to the loading zone in front and have their purchases carried out. Although the Co-op is not the place to go for, say, a pork roast, everything from household cleaning and personal care products to all foods except pork, beef, and lamb are available in a variety of choices. ➤

The Co-op's produce section is a mini farmers' market. For example, Garden Works, which has a booth at the Ann Arbor Farmers' Market, grows sunflower sprouts in a greenhouse and stores garlic in indoor flats, and sells them at the Co-op year 'round.

Some Ann Arborites may have puzzled over the steep hillside garden on the north side of Washtenaw a short distance east of the Washtenaw/East Stadium split. It seemed peculiarly large for a town garden. And it was. Until 1997 it was the garden of Duane Thomas, who now, with Judy Lobato, has a larger (and less visible) spot, Kestrel Farm, on Ann Arbor's west side. Thomas supplies the Co-op with a variety of produce, including lots of kale and collards favored by Sharon Barbour, who sautes them with garlic and tamari or soy sauce and serves them as a topping for brown rice. When spring comes, Co-op members know that the first local organic tomatoes to ripen will come from John Chamberlain's Bluebird Farm in Dexter. Norma and Dan Green specialize in shiitake mushrooms and also grow rhubarb, vegetables, and flowers. They welcome visitors (who should phone ahead at 734-663-4968) to their Green Acres Farm in Dexter. These growers are all members of the Organic Growers of Michigan, Southeast Chapter. Along with other members, they are listed in a membership directory available at the Co-op.

Organic apple grower Jane Bush of Charlotte, Michigan, brings cider, apple butter, and bottled apple sauce, priced to compete with commercial products. "Often organics cost more," Sharon Barbour told us, "but I think they often taste better because they're from smaller, better-tended farms." Organically grown garnet sweet potatoes were a case in point the day we were there. Top-shaped, smooth, and as beautiful as modern minimalist sculptures, they completely contradicted the old 1960's images of health food stores that sold pathetic looking produce. They were also more butterscotchy and delicious than the usual gnarled and dried-out supermarket sweet potatoes.

There's a huge range of bulk foods, including spices. Cheeses are a great buy at the Co-op, and the salad bar is a good source for pre-cut and washed veggies for stir-fries. The Co-op sells many locally baked breads, from bakers that include Ed's Breads, Depot Town Sourdough, Dockside Bakery, and Harvest Moon. We were lucky the day we were there because we got to meet Tom Burkman, co-owner of the Daily Grind, who was visiting the Co-op. The Daily Grind, which moved in 1977 from Ann Arbor to Mason, Michigan, supplies flour to the bakers of many of the Co-op breads. (Burkman had come in to buy some bread before heading back home after a business meeting.) He mills hard wheat flour for bread, soft wheat for pastries, Durham for pasta, and spelt for all three. (Spelt products are helpful for people with gluten allergies.) He also grinds cornmeal, rye flour, dark buckwheat, barley flour, and rice flour—all of which are for sale in the Co-op's bulk food section.

The Co-op carries delicious Calder milk in glass bottles. Whole milk yogurt with cream on top is another little-known treasure. The Co-op carries two brands—Brown Cow and Seven Stars. "The [Seven Stars] maple is so good," Barbour told us. "I can get the thirty-two ouncer and finish her up." We took her word for it. We tried it. In appreciation, we became Co-op members. ○

CHRISTINE PUDYK

An elfish spirit pervades the market. It's in the tickley smell of vegetables newly snapped from the vine, the gaudy ripeness of fruit, and the promise of satiety. Less obviously, some of it is emanating from stalls 77 and 78 in the tiny person of Christine Pudyk, whose last name appropriately evokes the sound of Pooh-ish, innocent impudence. The day we first met Pudyk, she was wearing a pale blue denim mushroom-shaped hat, from which wisps and curls of silver hair feathered out to surround a pair of mischievous brown eyes that simultaneously skewered and wooed us.

"I'm seventy-five years old," she said.

"Why do you still come to market?" we asked.

"Because I'm stupid," she replied.

"How did you get into farming?" we asked.

"By mistake," she said.

And the conversation continued teasingly for a while until we found that interspersed with the merriment was a story of hard times mitigated by the kind of humor and love of life that gets a person through thick and thin and, sometimes, thin and thin. Pudyk came to the U.S. from the Ukraine in 1947, only after enduring the horrors that preceded and surrounded World War II. They are likely to come up in reminiscences about characters Pudyk knew and events she witnessed. But for the last twenty-five years she has been farming six acres on Pontiac Trail, north of Ann Arbor, and bringing flowers and vegetables to market.

"She's the best," said a loyal customer who stopped by for cucumbers. "I come here every week!"

The customer got five huge cucumbers for $1. "I sell like I would pay for it myself," Pudyk says. "I wouldn't pay more than a dollar for five or six cucumbers." A big zucchini (Pudyk regretted its large size, since the smaller ones are less pulpy) was 35 cents and a box of small ones was $1, as was a huge bunch of Spanish onions.

How does Pudyk cook zucchini? "Well," she says, looking embarrassed but sing-songing out the truth, "for m-e-e-e-e, when I do-o-o-o-o, it's not too healthy. I peel it, I slice it, I flour it and dip in egg and crumbs, and then fr-r-r-y it in Crisco." This is followed by a tilt of the head, a beatific grin— implied advice to enjoy life's small pleasures wherever they show up. ⭕

RENAISSANCE ACRES
PETER AND KRIS STARK

Energetic Peter Stark and his creative wife, Kris, own an organic herb farm meaningfully named Renaissance Acres and romantically located on Valentine Road, a few miles north of Ann Arbor. They bring potted herbs, some vegetables, and starter herb plants to the Farmers' Market.

Most of the market farmers, certainly the older ones, come from farming families, but Peter Stark is one of the varied group who came to farming through idealism. Fifteen-some hard years of practical hard work haven't diminished his ardor; he seems always to have time to explain or discuss the merits of a particular herb or the reasons to use one farming method or another. As a guitar-playing college student in the 1970's, he made his own course plan in order to study what was then called "alternative" farming and is now more usually called "organic" farming. After leaving school in the late 1970's, he helped in the creation of the People's Food Co-op.

In 1979, Stark turned to actual farming, buying a twenty-acre property that had been a dairy until the 1940's and had lain fallow since. How did an ex-folk singer know how to turn a neglected property into a very trim and tidy farm?

"I started on a shoestring and planted three acres with only an eight-horsepower Troy-bilt rototiller," he says. "I grew up in Saginaw, and my parents had a big garden. My grandmother always had apple trees and she also made her own root beer. . . . You learn by your mistakes and there are fluctuations, but if you work hard enough and are persistent enough, the human can do almost anything." He immediately put his knowledge and commitment to organic farming to work. "It's something I'm trying to do for the planet," he says. Then, worried that that may sound pretentious, he quickly adds, "This is just a little corner, and I don't do it to influence other people, but maybe some twenty-year-old will see it and do it, too."

In addition to their market business, the Starks have sales hours at their farm. Kris produces a detailed catalog for phone, write-in or email purchases. The catalog offers over 500 varieties of herbs and thirty varieties of organic vegetable starter plants. (It also includes beeswax candles, bath and body oils, and bath herbs that Kris assembles, during summer evenings and winter days, in the family's 100-year-old farmhouse.) Peter brings a huge number of plants to the market and can explain both their nutritive value and their use.

"Rosemary," he explains, for example, "is good with any kind of potato—baked, boiled, steamed; a little fresh thyme in a salad just gives it that bouquet; French tarragon added to spaghetti sauce gives an anise undertone; borage tastes like cucumber, and you can use it in salads; upland cress tastes like watercress, but you don't need running water to grow it—you can grow it on high ground—and it's the highest of all vegetables in Vitamin E." ○

CATHERINE AND ED RESKE

Farming is Catherine Reske's post-retirement career! She describes herself as a "stay-at-home mom" who trained as a Licensed Practical Nurse after the kids were grown. Then, about twenty years ago, Catherine and her husband, Ed, who is an over-the-road trucker, decided to buy a small farm near Manchester. They named it Reske's Herb and Honey Farm. In June, when strawberries are ripe, the farm is open to people who want to come and pick their own berries. Although it might sound easier to keep their farm open all summer than to haul produce to market, Catherine says it's "grueling to have people coming eight or nine hours a day, seven days a week." So she comes to the Farmers' Market Wednesdays and Saturdays from April through November.

Catherine Reske comes from a food-oriented family. Her grandfather was a sausage maker in Poland and her father continued the family trade in Detroit. Her heritage and training have given her a life-long appreciation of quality, a nurse's awareness of nutrition, a gardener's love of produce, a mother's concern for care, and a natural sense of beauty. Her appreciation and knowledge of leeks, for example, show how much all these factors come into play in her farming, her cooking, and the products she brings to market.

"Once you cook with leeks, you love them," she says. "The flavor is mild and delicate. It's wonderful. Do you know that leeks are the national emblem of Wales? People don't realize how much work leeks are [to grow]. We start the seeds in the greenhouse. It takes a hundred and twenty growing days from seed to seedling. A seedling looks like a blade of grass. You hand-plant them as deep as you can—six to ten inches, usually, so just a tip of green is sticking out of the ground. Then later [when they've grown taller], you hill them—you build a hill of dirt around them. The higher the soil around them, the more white part there'll be. We have nice sandy loam. We're in a fertile valley, but if there's a drought we're in trouble, so we use some drip irrigation.

"In the fall, I use leeks for potato soup—I have a heart-smart recipe, no cream. I also use them in clean-out-the-refrigerator soup. I use the leek right up to where it branches, but you can also use the rest of the green for soup stock. To store leeks for winter, I just wash them, chop them, and freeze them in plastic bags; that way they're all ready to use." Even the core left over from making stuffed cabbage gets the chop-and-freeze treatment for future use in soup stock. "The core," Reske says, "has a wonderful sweet flavor."

Reske has two acres of asparagus planted for spring marketing. Summers, she has the complete range of vegetables. Her favorite tomatoes are the oval Italian or Roma variety. "People want that picture-perfect tomato," she says, "but the Italian is a wonderful all-purpose tomato. The flavor is unique, and they don't spoil as readily." By planting twice, she can bring broccoli in both July and September. Honey, available from the Reskes from August on, is a by-product of the hives Ed keeps to ensure plant pollination. In the fall Catherine brings bountiful dried holiday arrangements in dreamy colors made from grasses and flowers she has grown and dried during the summer. ◯

"I love watching things grow, and when people buy the stuff, it's an added bonus," Catherine Reske says.

RALPH SNOW

STORAGE TIP

Once opened, maple sugar products should be refrigerated to prevent the growth of molds.

COOKING TIP

We saw Snow learn something from a customer, who came by for two half-pound bags of maple sugar. She said she uses 1/3 cup of honey and 1/2 cup of maple sugar in place of 1 1/2 cups of sugar in her banana bread and other fruit-based quick breads for healthier products that, she says, have a butterscotch taste.

"My great-granddad did this in the eighteen-hundreds, and we're still tapping the same trees," says Ralph Snow of Mason, about fifty miles northwest of Ann Arbor. "You have to have hard maple trees; they give a good sugar content and the sap is not bitter." Even his newer trees descend from his great-granddad's maples. Hard maples self-seed so abundantly that the trick is to thin them out properly rather than to plant more.

Sap production varies enormously from year to year depending on weather conditions. The yield can also depend on the maple tapper's ability to guess when to start the tap. Snow was pleased with his call for 1997. He decided to tap on February 15. During southeastern Michigan's great ice storm on March 23 that year, other growers' trees, still under pressure from heavy loads of sap, snapped under the weight of the ice. The Snow family, however, was already boiling sap, so not only did they realize 1997's yield, but also their unburdened trees were light and flexible enough to withstand the ice.

Once gathered, the watery yield is reduced in a 16 foot by 16 foot evaporator. It takes forty gallons of sap to make one pound of maple syrup. Maple sugar, from further concentration of the syrup, is delicious used in place of white sugar, and it's so concentrated that only a little will do. The Snow family makes maple sugar candy by heating the syrup to 242 degrees and then pouring it into molds ranging from maple leaf to Santa Claus shapes. A very special treat is their maple cream, made by heating maple syrup to 232 degrees, quickly chilling it, and then whipping it into a flaxen-pale spread for toast, biscuits, and bread.

In addition to coming to market year 'round, Snow wholesales maple sugar products. His biggest project, though, and the one that brings a gleam to his eye, is Snow's Sugarbush, the breakfast restaurant he and his family run in Mason, Thursdays through Saturdays from February 15 to April 15. For $4.99, it's an all-you-can-eat buffet in a big pole barn that seats 350 people. Snow says the place is so popular that customers almost always have to wait to be seated. The buffet features old-time country dishes like buttermilk pancakes, Texas-style French toast, Belgian waffles, and whole-hog sausage specially made in Kansas City. Needless to say, there's lot's of maple syrup, maple sugar, and maple cream to top things off.

Snow also packs and sends Christmas boxes, which sell so well by word of mouth that he doesn't advertise them at all. They run from $18 to $50 plus postage. ○

SPARROW MEAT MARKET
BOB SPARROW

Few contemporary supermarket butchers ever see whole animals. Supermarkets purchase meat by the box—roasts in one box, steaks in another, etc., all coming from many animals.

Bob Sparrow, owner of Sparrow Meat Market, however, buys whole hanging beef, veal, and lamb and does all the butchering on site. He thinks only one or two other Ann Arbor butchers follow this traditional method—Knight's Market on Miller is one he knows of for sure.

Sparrow's loyal customers are fully aware that they're getting great meat, but they may not know exactly why they prefer it to almost any other. Sparrow explains that from inspection through cutting and wrapping, the traditional butchering method provides a much better product. Solid craftsmanship is a way of life he was taught as a child.

"My grandpa had a feed mill in Willis. I grew up on a farm there," he says. "Most of our animals went to the stockyard, but we slaughtered for our own use. I was also a hunter and a trapper from the time I was a kid. I worked part-time in a butcher shop when I was in high school. When I was twenty-two I heard the butcher shop at South Main Market was for sale, and I bought it. My mom [Ginny Sparrow] quit her beauty shop job to come help me out there. I bought this two years later. Business here was better, and my mom wanted to stop, so we sold the South Main Market store last year." (To the delight of customers who knew her at the South Main Market, Ginny Sparrow puts in some hours at Sparrow's in Kerrytown.)

"Buying whole animals is a lot more work," Bob Sparrow says, "but it makes for far better quality. I work seventy or eighty hours a week and I haven't had a vacation for fourteen years. I've got great guys working for me—they've all been here ten, twelve years. The meat is fresh, not sealed in a bag for days, as it is at the supermarket."

Sparrow and his staff prepare traditional cuts such as pot roast with the bone in (for rich flavor), beef shanks, and meaty short ribs. Delicate veal, especially, profits from fine butchering and handling, and Sparrow sells a lot of it—from apple-stuffed roasts to succulent scaloppine. He sells only prime grade lamb, most of it from Michigan. Cuts range from elegant crown roasts to flavorful lamb patties. Beef, of course, ranges from hearty steak to thinly sliced "sukiyaki" beef, which is great for stir fries and other recipes where a minimal amount of meat can pack a big punch. Sparrow also carries dressed rabbit, known for its plumpness and flavor, and big, meaty boneless duck breasts. ➤

Amish chickens are kept on ice for absolute freshness rather than, as he says, "wrapped in a package somewhere in Arkansas." Sparrow sells Danish bacon almost as brightly colored as a barber pole; in Denmark, he says, hogs are fed slowly, which makes the bacon meatier. Recently, Sparrow began offering fragrant beef, veal, chicken, and lamb stock, cooked at the shop. He's also preparing some ready-made foods, including a delicately textured chicken salad that exemplifies his ability to retain the moist goodness of meat during cooking; the instructions he gives to his customers always emphasize ways to do that.

"People who shop here [Kerrytown] are more food-oriented than most," Sparrow says, "and they want to make their own recipes. But there are also a lot of people with little time who want things ready to cook. We've tried oodles and oodles of semi-prepared things." The most successful, besides the burgers and the fabulous fruit-, vegetable-, and herb-stuffed roasts, is a line of chicken sausages variously combined with raspberries, Portobello mushrooms, apples, and tomato with garlic. Sparrow does special cuts and special orders and is unfailing in unpretentious service and superb quality. ○

LOUISE & DAVE ST. CLAIR AND LELA ALBER

Most of the market growers are truck farmers only—they grow produce in small enough quantities to truck to market themselves. Louise St. Clair, however, is part of a crop farming family. In addition to a truck garden, the family plants or rents out about 650 acres of feed corn, soybeans, and alfalfa for hay. A truck farm makes more per acre, but is constant, perfectionist work. A crop farm requires a lot of acres, a lot of heavy equipment and muscle, and a lot of know-how.

"A bushel of feed corn might get about three dollars a bushel at the elevator," St. Clair points out, "but it can get a little more [at the market] when it's for squirrels." As U.S. farm operations continue to favor larger-scale farming, she and her family are in the process of figuring out whether the next generation can support itself as the preceding two have on their Saline farm—whether by crop farming, truck farming, or a combination of the two.

"My great-grandparents farmed in this area. My mom and dad, Elmer and Lela Alber, started the farm we have now," St. Clair says. In addition to cash crop farming, they kept dairy cows and took steers to market. St. Clair's grown daughters, son, and daughter-in-law are doing lots of the heavy work now. Though they've given up the dairy farming, they still keep pigs and "thirty or so" steers.

"I can remember Mom driving an old steel-wheel tractor before there were rubber wheels," St. Clair recalls. "I love to drive the tractor, too." At eighty-three, Lela Alber still washes and bundles produce for the market. She bags spinach and a salad mix. She also shells lima beans. It takes about fifteen minutes to do a pint, which sells for $3.

A typical farm day, St. Clair says, starts with getting breakfast and doing morning chores. In July, she'll get out in the garden before it gets too hot. Weeding is a favorite chore. "It's satisfying," she says, "to see a row looking nice. You have to love this [farming] to do it, because the monetary reward isn't great. In the middle of the week, I pick things for my own freezer. On a nice day, quitting time could be nine or ten o'clock at night. Getting-ready-for-market-days are harder than farming days. We pick everything the day before."

Does she worry about losses due to weather or pests? "No, and we don't use sprays," St. Clair says. "When you plant, you just plant a little extra. We have such a diverse variety that you figure some things will work [even if others don't]. This [1997] was a cool year and the tomatoes took forever to ripen, but the peas were wonderful."

St. Clair has helped with a cookbook, too. The second edition of the fund-raiser cookbook for St. John's Lutheran Church in Bridgewater came out in 1996. It can be purchased at the Alber-St.Clair stall for $10. It includes Lela Alber's recipes for lebkuchen and for a cherry salad. Louise St. Clair's recipes include holiday macaroons, apple crisp, and homemade noodles. ○

TIP
Louise St. Clair says lima beans are best when they're "a good green color, not white. When they get too big, they get white and starchy."

TRACKLEMENTS
T. R. DURHAM

"It's dense, resilient, and buttery, and it maintains its integrity and fresh flavor in a variety of dishes. The reason is the long cold cure with hand-rubbed dry, rather than brine, cure," says T. R. Durham, describing his smoked salmon.

"Along the coasts of Ireland and Scotland, almost every little town has an operation like this," says T. R. Durham, owner of Durham's Tracklements, a smokery located in the Kerrytown Market Building (its door is on Kingsley, on the north edge of the complex). Sandy-haired and leprechaun charming, Durham might have just arrived from one of those coasts. Where he did arrive from is Amherst, Massachusetts, and not so long ago.

Tracklements was a thriving business with Manhattan accounts that included Balducci's and Dean and DeLuca when, in 1996, T. R.'s wife was offered a faculty position at the U-M. They decided to make the move as a family, but T. R. had some thinking to do about whether or not to move his business. It meant not only distancing himself from his prestigious New York outlets, but also moving equipment or buying new, and it meant a move away from his Atlantic Coast fish suppliers.

Monahan's Fish Market figured big in Durham's decision. He rates Monahan's fish purchasing and handling right up there with the top-notch coastal fish markets. So he not only decided to move the business to Ann Arbor, but he decided to move it to Kerrytown in order to buy fresh fish in cooperation with Monahan's and to use the fish shop as part of his retailing plan. After months of negotiations with suppliers, Monahan and Durham arranged for fresh salmon to be flown in each week direct from the same Bay of Fundy farm that had supplied Tracklements in Massachusetts. The business moved just fine. Tracklements Thai Smoked Salmon had made the New York Times 1995 Best Mail Order Gifts list, compiled by food maven Marian Burros. Within a few months of moving here in 1997, Tracklements made the list again, with Burros praising the little company's Scottish Highland, Thai, and Provencal specialty salmon cures. Small wonder—the fish is fabulous.

On a trip to Scotland in 1984, Durham rented a cottage in the northwest highlands. The cottage manager, Duncan Stewart, smoked fish for restaurants and hotels in the highland area. Stewart agreed to let Durham work along with him for the six weeks of his vacation. Durham returned to Scotland in 1986 to learn more and then began experimenting in earnest back home. He sent samples of his work to a brother in Kansas City—a big barbecue town, but relatively deprived in matters of salmon. Impressed, his brother offered to put up half the money for Durham's first smokery. T. R. named it Tracklements after an adaptation by British folklorist and cookbook writer Dorothy Hartley, who had altered "trucklement," a colloquialism for "a bit of something" or "an accompaniment."

Durham smokes many kinds of fish and duck, and on the day we visited he was even smoking balls of fresh mozzarella for a special customer. But his main product is smoked salmon. Unlike most smoked salmon available in the Midwest, Durham's salmon is cold-smoked after being hand-rubbed with kosher or sea salt, brown sugar, and blends of herbs and spices for unique specialty cures. The alternative way of smoking salmon is to soak it in salt brine and then to smoke it at high temperatures. Brine cure is a traditional method that also produces a fine product, though completely different in taste and texture. Hand-rubbed cures and slow-cure low temperature smoking makes what T. R. calls a "dense and buttery" product. "It's essentially drying in the presence of smoke," he explains. It's great for eating on bread or crackers, and it's unmatched for salads, pasta dishes, or even pizzas and sushis.

There are two reasons this style of smoking hasn't been common around here. One is that it requires more time and skill and the other is that from the mid-1960's until 1997, the technique was not allowed by Michigan's Department of Agriculture. The explanation was a panic that occurred in the mid-1960's when a truckload of hot-smoked fish (not from Michigan) overturned in the South. The fish was recovered and sold, after some time sitting in the sun it caused an outbreak of botulism—and an outbreak of hasty legislation. Durham's consideration of a Michigan move came at the same time that the state reconsidered its policy, so Tracklements was able to become the first cold-smoker in Michigan in thirty years.

T. R. Durham fits right into the pantheon of food-district craftsmen. He is entirely occupied by his work. He loves to talk about it. He loves the approval of happy customers. And he loves to experiment. "Hand-rubbing and slow smoking gives you a chance to be more creative," he says. "You can do a variety of herbs, spices, salts, and salt and sugar combinations." His Thai Smoked Salmon, for example, is "infused with ginger, coriander, and mixed aromatic peppercorns and a hint of lemon grass, then smoked over fruitwoods and tea." Highland Smoked Salmon is "cured with sea salt, evaporated sugar cane juice, and malt whiskey and lightly smoked over oak, applewood, and alder."

After rubbing, the fish is cured for somewhere between thirty-six and ninety-six hours, depending on the recipe, then smoked at temperatures between 70 and 90 degrees Fahrenheit for ten to sixteen hours. It's then cooled and vacuum-packed. (This doesn't cover the entire process—T. R., who generally likes to share, admits he has a couple of secret steps he's not going to divulge.) Packaged, the fish can be kept in the refrigerator for up to three weeks, or frozen for up to four months. An open package can be kept in the refrigerator for up to a week. This flexibility makes it a delicacy that can be kept on hand.

Because Tracklements fish is available hand-sliced at Monahan's Fish Market, the Kingsley Street shop is open only a few midday hours on Wednesday, Friday, and Saturday. Saturday features tastings and wonderful take-out smoked salmon sushi. (The toll-free mail order phone number is 800-844-7853; the local number is 930-6642.) Durham enjoys his shop hours because they give him a chance to discuss recipes for his smoked fish and duck. His suggestions run the gamut from confit and cassoulet of duck to sushi made with salmon. One tasty idea: mix chopped smoked salmon with capers, crushed black pepper, and a squeeze of lemon juice; serve on crackers or bread rounds. ◯

WASEM FRUIT FARM
LEOLA WASEM AND
JAN & BRUCE UPSTON

TIP

The Golden Russet apple, Leola Wasem says, is an example of a tasty old-fashioned apple that can be purchased at the Farmers' Market, but that doesn't do well in grocery stores because it doesn't' have a tidy look. Northern Spy, she adds, "is the best pie apple."

"I married a fellow from Columbus," Leola Wasem says. "He was a city fellow, but he liked farming. He worked for Argus Camera." (The company had a plant on Ann Arbor's west side.) Leola and Ed Wasem were married in 1942. While Ed spent the day at Argus, Leola worked with her parents and her twin brother, Lee, on the family farm on Judd Road, south of Ypsilanti, near the present Wasem farm. Ed loved to farm, Leola says, so he not only helped at Wasem farms, he helped out other farmers, too.

"We used to take a hundred dressed chickens to the market during the war," Wasem recalls. "Other meat was rationed, but not chickens. At that time, it wasn't hard to get a stall. Now there's a waiting list." Many things have changed. Wasem, now in her eighties and still full of youthful energy, doesn't bring chickens anymore. Ed died eleven years ago, and their daughter and son-in-law, Jan and Bruce Upston, have joined her in farming and at the market. Besides produce, they bring baked goods and jam that Wasem makes for market and for sale at Wasem's Fruit Farm, where people can also pick their own fruit.

"I'd always said I'd never make jam, I'd never bake [for the market]," says Wasem, who majored in hospital dietetics at Michigan State. "The reason I started was we had acres and acres of peaches. They were delicious, but they got too ripe. It [making jam and baking] wasn't as bad I thought it would be. In the fall, we also make up to two hundred dozen doughnuts a day. Everything's automatic. I get everything ready the night before." She also bakes cookies and quick breads. Most of her jams are made from Wasem-grown fruit, but she also makes some tropical varieties for which she buys pineapples and kiwis. "Chutney and butters [like apple butter] that take a lot of cooking, I do when it's cool.

"It's a six-day-a-week job," she says. "Seven days in the fall, when we don't take a day off for two months. On market day we leave home at four-forty in the morning in the summers and five-thirty or so in the winter. In the fall, we leave at three-thirty because we have so much to unload. I go to bed at nine. It's better to work than not to work. I cannot sit down and not do anything."

Wasem and the Upstons come to the Farmers' Market year 'round, and the calendar dictates what they bring, except for the baked goods and jam they always have. During the coldest months, they bring cider and apples that have been held in cold storage since late autumn. In March and April they add pussy willow branches; in May they add cut rhubarb and starter roots and bulbs for rhubarb, iris, lily-of-the-valley, violets, and other spring plants. Sometimes cherries are ready by late June. In July it's time for currents and

peas. By late August, in addition to vegetables, the peaches and early apples will come in. September is when Wasem's orchards reach their true glory, with apples, peaches, plums, pears, fall raspberries, pumpkins, and squash.

The fruit farm is open for fall apple picking, and schedules of expected prime times for various varieties are available at the family's market stall during September and October. The family also provides tours for groups and for classes of children between the ages of three and eight. Leola Wasem estimates that between 2,000 and 3,000 children come every year. For Wasem's Fruit Farms shop hours, to find out what's in season, or to schedule a tour, call (734) 482-2342. ○

BILL WEST

"It's horrid to pick, it tastes putrid, but it's in demand," says okra grower Bill West, who's earned a special niche by growing something most local farmers don't bother with at all. Okra is a hard sell in Michigan. It is rarely served in northern U.S. restaurants, which means that people not already familiar with okra—a cone-shaped vegetable with a gluey (slimy, one could say)—texture aren't likely to learn about it.

But okra's scarcity is just what makes it popular with West. Folks who do know how to use it also know that one of the few places where they can get it fresh and picked small is at his stall at the Ann Arbor Farmers' Market. Michiganders do happily eat okra when they go to New Orleans. It is one of the basic ingredients, and the thickening agent for, gumbo soup. The word "gumbo" itself derives from the African word for okra. It's also widely used in the Middle East, India, and China, so West has a culturally diverse bunch of loyal customers for his boxes of vegetables that look like pointy heads with ribbed, green stocking caps. Okra pods grow on woody plants that reach over 6 feet in height by the end of summer. West has to bend the stalks down in order to pick the pods. To make things worse, the stalks are itchy, he says.

Fortunately, while West was telling us just how terrible okra is, customer Natasha Flyer stopped to buy some. Flyer told us how delicious it is and just how to cook it, according to traditions she learned from her Turkish grandmother.

West's okra discourse is good-humored. At 6 feet 5 inches, he's an uncommonly handsome thirty-six-year-old who chose, rather than inherited, the farming life. It was a way to be an entrepreneur and to be outdoors as well. "I started going to market with the guy across the road, somewhere between twelve and fifteen years ago when I was in high school," he says. "My parents had cattle, but didn't sell vegetables." He eventually built up his own vegetable business and built a greenhouse for his seedlings. "Everything I grow, I start myself," he says.

Besides the maligned okra, West sells large quantities of more common fare. He estimates that for each market day at the height of the season he'll pick and sell about thirty bushels of tomatoes, ten of green beans, and five bushels each of two different kinds of eggplant. A bushel of beans, for example, takes about an hour to pick and will bring him about $30. "Picking is kind of hard," he admits, "but the market is fun. If I don't succeed, it's my fault— not somebody else's." ○

BOB WISE

Bob Wise is probably the only one of the Farmers' Market growers who raises outdoor crops all year 'round. He spends his summers in the Ann Arbor area, growing vegetables and taking them to market. From September through April, he does the same thing in Florida. He is also probably the only grower who makes Windsor chairs. He makes thirty each winter and sells them in Florida.

Farming isn't Wise's first career. Up until a few years ago, he worked as a respiratory therapist. Gardening was a hobby that became more and more important to him until he finally simply changed careers. He has been specializing in Chinese greens, in part because they give him a specialty niche, in part because he likes them, and in part because they are quite heat-tolerant. The greens are quick growing. When he gets to his seasonal habitat, whichever it is, he can get the seed in the ground and be at market a month later, whereas pokier green beans take about fifty days.

A quiet man, Wise posts signs over each of his unusual vegetables, explaining what each is and how each should be cooked, but if a customer wants to know more, he'll enthusiastically explain what the greens are and how they can be used. Most of the greens, he says, are good cooked in stir-fries or raw in salads. They include komatsuna, a Japanese mustard spinach; choy sun, a big green with small yellow flowers that are also edible; and baby Chinese cabbage.

West also grows several kinds of green beans, including slim French beans, or haricots verts, which offer a big taste in reverse proportion to their delicate, slender size. He grows a variety of cherry tomato called Sweet 100, of which he says, "People know it like they know Kleenex is tissue." Admitting that his Brandywine tomatoes are "cosmetically ugly," he adds that the delicious old-fashioned variety doesn't sacrifice flavor for shelf life as so many contemporary hybrids do. ○

ZINGERMAN'S DELI AND ZINGERMAN'S PRACTICAL PRODUCE
PAUL SAGINAW & ARI WEINZWEIG

The alphabet conspires to place Zingerman's Deli last in the list of food purveyors in the Ann Arbor Farmers' Market area. In national fame, Zingerman's is first. Articles about and references to Zingerman's Deli, Zingerman's Bakehouse, and owners Paul Saginaw and Ari Weinzweig appear regularly in national newspapers and magazines, including *Bon Appétit* and *Eating Well*. Nevertheless, it was just our modest friends Paul and Ari, who sat with us on separate days and talked about Zingerman's, about food, and about good living, which all came out to be pretty much the same thing.

It should be said that Zingerman's has other owners, too. It has been Paul and Ari's practice to share ownership in each of the business's segments with their managers. Their old friend Frank Carollo co-owns the Bakehouse, which he developed. Tommy York is a managing partner in the deli. Maggie Baylis is a partner in ZingTrain, an offshoot of Zingerman's own staff training program that is now Zingerman's training and consulting arm, offering seminars and training to other food specialty stores and to other organizations, including the University of Michigan Library.

When Saginaw and Weinzweig opened the deli in 1982, they were certainly not the business and food authorities they are today. (More precisely, Zingerman's was founded by close friends Mike Monahan and Saginaw, then co-owners of Monahan's Fish Market at Kerrytown, with Weinzweig as managing partner; some years later, Monahan bought Saginaw's share of the fish market and Saginaw bought Monahan's interest in the deli.) Their qualifications were a handful of assorted college degrees, experience working at a local restaurant, good intentions, fairly strong backs, and, best of all, curiosity. "I had no intention of going into the food business," Weinzweig says. "I never knew you go into business at all. I'm from a family of teachers, doctors, and lawyers. I'm the failure—I don't have an advanced degree. Now I'm a CEO [chief executive officer]; it's like being a dishwasher."

They first leased and later bought a nifty little red brick building at the corner of Detroit Street and Kingsley. In hindsight, the decision looks brilliant. At the time, it seemed pretty dim. Although neighborhood grocery stores had survived there, another deli operation had tried and failed. And even though Ann Arborites clamored for delis, those that started at other locations had failed, too. But Zingerman's Deli worked from the very beginning. Saginaw and Weinzweig turned out to be the Rodgers and Hammerstein of the deli business.

Their bywords seemed to be "more" and "better." As soon as they raised a little capital (and sometimes even before that) they'd buy more product. As soon as the service became very good, Saginaw and Weinzweig went to work to make it excellent.

As Weinzweig expanded his knowledge of food, he also increased his visits to food craftsmen and suppliers all over the world. "The more I learned about food, the more I loved it," he recalls. "It wasn't an epiphany. I started reading cookbooks and meeting [food] people." He started writing about food, too, until today the newsletter that the cashier offers customers at checkout is the finest free food ink around. It features philosophy, as in "One of my most passionate beliefs about food is that the simplest dishes are almost always the most enjoyable." It offers advice:"This time of the year [January/February] your best bet will be the vine-on-tomatoes from Holland or Israel." And it dangles succulent enticements: "Heather honey has a flavor with just a touch of toasted toffee, a pinch of perfume, a hint of the Scottish hills. Try rubbing a leg of lamb with a blend of heather honey and apple cider." That's Ari Weinzweig, the almond-hued, almond-eyed romantic.

Paul is more matzo ball than almond—round, warm, lovable, but with overtones of ancestral anxiety. "Paul, anything new that we start, he's full-bore in there to get it going," Weinzweig told us. Having succeeded beyond dreams with the deli and the bakehouse, the partners decided a good produce store should be possible, too. They bought an existing, rather unexciting, produce business at Kerrytown to see what they could do. Paul has applied the Zingerman's concept of abundance and quality and turned the place into a vibrant market with a loyal clientele. Saginaw and Weinzweig are still experimenting with its concept.

Weinzweig would like to see it specialize in Latin American food products. In early 1998, they already had the largest local offering of products like masa, which is corn flour mixed with lime for making tortillas, and they're selling prepared tortilla soup, tamales, quesadillas, and chiles relenos. No matter what its emphasis, it will be eclectic. Like the deli, the produce store carries the output of Zingerman's Bakehouse, the breads and the pies, cakes, and other pastries that turn amber waves of grain into golden puffs of physical and emotional sustenance.

The Zingerman's mail order catalog is a delight just to read. It's also a fine way to send presents to friends and relatives living in places without an equally good deli (in other words, everywhere). Call 888-636-8162 for a free catalog. Then you'll be able to order Zingerman's Guide to Good Olive Oil, good olive oil, membership in the Zingerman's bread club with monthly delivery,"real Italian tuna," a Reuben sandwich kit (all the makings for four giant sandwiches), fine caviar, and many more of life's essentials.

The impact of the Zingerman's phenomenon extends far beyond Ann Arbor. But it's only here, in the vicinity of the Farmers' Market, that one can walk into the garlic-laden air of Zingerman's, make a spur-of-the-moment purchase of a bottle of truffle oil, sample a delicious imported cheese, or stop Ari Weinzweig for a personal consultation about olive oil, vinegar, or, metaphorically or literally, schmaltz. ○

INDEX

ORDERING INFORMATION

TO ORDER COPIES OF *ANN ARBOR FRESH!*,
SEND $20.45
(FOR MICHIGAN RESIDENTS, $21.38) TO:
KITCHEN PORT
415 NORTH FIFTH AVENUE
ANN ARBOR, MI 48104

OR TO ORDER BY PHONE AND PAY BY CREDIT CARD,
CALL 1-800-832-7678
(POSTAGE FOR ORDERS OUTSIDE THE U.S.
IS SOMEWHAT HIGHER)